GLOBAL SEX

GLOBAL SEX

What Sex Workers Know About Love And Capitalism

Sine Plambech

Translated from the Danish by Michael Favala Goldman

akoya

LONDON

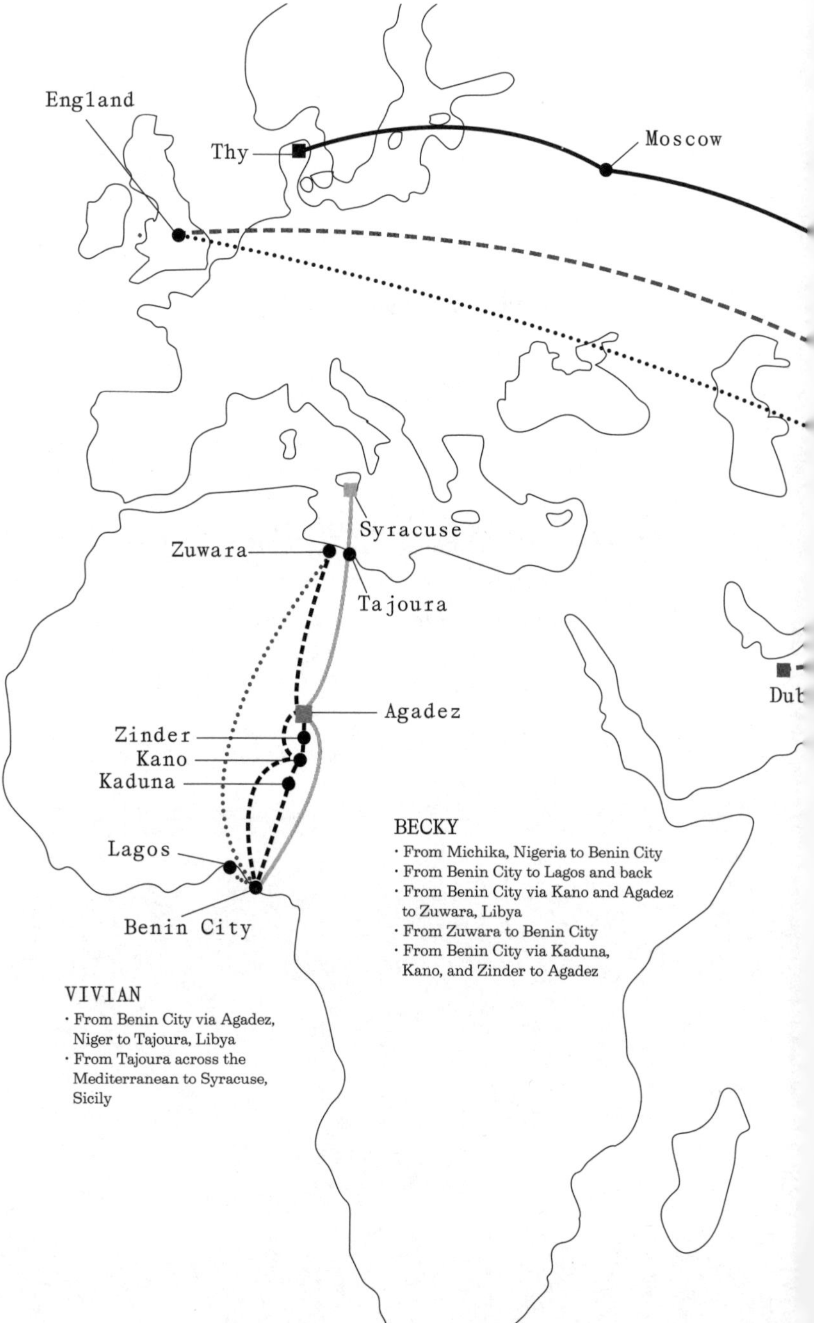
England
Thy
Moscow
Syracuse
Zuwara
Tajoura
Dub
Agadez
Zinder
Kano
Kaduna
Lagos
Benin City
BECKY
· From Michika, Nigeria to Benin City
· From Benin City to Lagos and back
· From Benin City via Kano and Agadez to Zuwara, Libya
· From Zuwara to Benin City
· From Benin City via Kaduna, Kano, and Zinder to Agadez
VIVIAN
· From Benin City via Agadez, Niger to Tajoura, Libya
· From Tajoura across the Mediterranean to Syracuse, Sicily

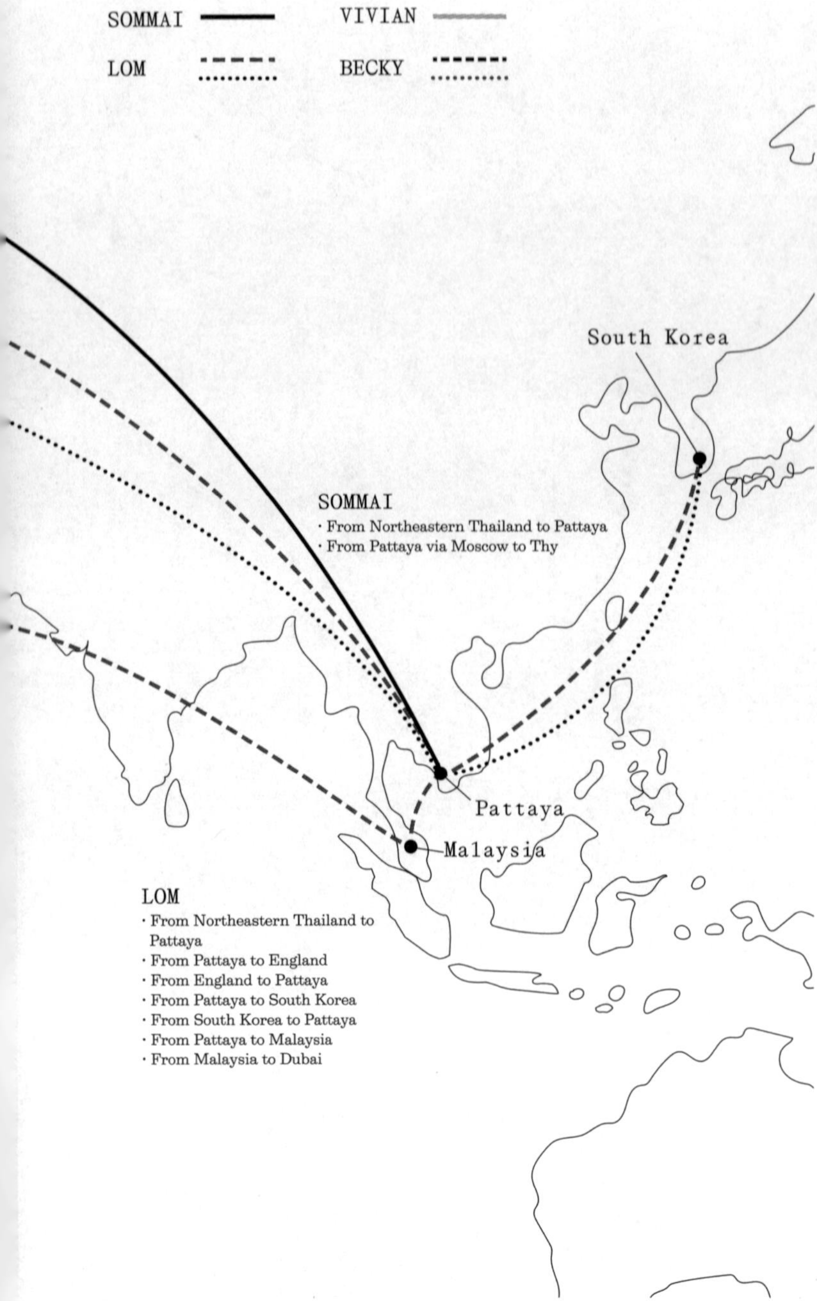
SOMMAI
VIVIAN
LOM
BECKY
South Korea
SOMMAI
· From Northeastern Thailand to Pattaya
· From Pattaya via Moscow to Thy
Pattaya
Malaysia
LOM
· From Northeastern Thailand to Pattaya
· From Pattaya to England
· From England to Pattaya
· From Pattaya to South Korea
· From South Korea to Pattaya
· From Pattaya to Malaysia
· From Malaysia to Dubai

Foreword

Dear readers,

You might think a book about sex workers has little to do with your own experiences, but this book concerns us all – the stories in *Global Sex* are ours too. As the title suggests, sex is a commodity that is sold worldwide – by women and men, cisgender and transgender. In this book, you will meet four women. Mothers, sisters, daughters, sex workers. Women you might pass on the street, women who might be your friends, generously telling you what the world looks like from their perspective. I invite you to join us in the rooms, feelings and hearts that are often hidden from public view.

Everything you are about to read is partly informed by the sphere of my own context. *Global Sex* is a deeply personal book, in which I draw on the past twenty years of my life as an anthropologist among people and communities who often exist under the radar. I'm from Denmark – I have lived and worked here on and off over the years, and some of the stories in the book have a specific connection to the landscape of the Danish sex industry. But research which, for me, began in Copenhagen, has taken me all over the world, and the stories shared here are both specific to my experiences and encounters, and reflective of a much larger picture of interconnected global trade.

Due to the hidden nature of sex work, it is difficult to accurately estimate the number of sex workers in any country, but we know that in Denmark, approximately

80 per cent of sex workers are migrant women, mostly from Thailand, Nigeria and Eastern Europe. In the UK, there are an estimated 102,000 sex workers and, as in Denmark and throughout most of the world, the majority are women. However, in contrast to Denmark, in the UK the ratio of citizens to migrants selling sex is 50:50, and the majority of those migrants are from Eastern Europe.

The differences or similarities between our countries, however, are not the main point of *Global Sex*. Rather, this book highlights that all the women working in red-light districts around the world – Soho in London, Sheil Road in Liverpool, Istedgade in Denmark, De Wallen in Amsterdam, Pattaya in Thailand – are connected through lived experience. When you walk through these neighbourhoods, I hope you will remember that these women are more than the stigmatised figure of 'the prostitute', 'the whore', 'the sex-slave'. They are humans with lives and longings like all of us.

Living and working on the edge of the law creates a dilemma, and legislation around sex work is a key factor impacting sex workers' livelihoods. In the UK, it is legal to exchange sex for money, but other related activities such as running brothels, street work and advertising sexual services are criminalised, so anything a sex worker does to contact a client puts them at risk.

Sex workers need to be visible to get clients and make money, but at the same time must stay hidden so that they don't end up on the wrong side of the law. Organisations such as the English Collective of Prostitutes have linked national austerity policies to a rise in sex work, and the Department for Work and Pensions recognises the link between welfare reforms and 'survival sex', a term used to describe the exchange of sexual services to meet basic needs. Living under the radar not only makes your life dangerous, it also makes you invisible to the support that could keep you safe. The women in this book will show you what it means to live a precarious life.

Brexit has also had particularly negative consequences for EU migrant workers, including increased risk of arrest and deportation. While courts have allowed sex workers from the EU to claim self-employed status and remain in the UK, there is no established case law. And since sex work is not recognised as a legitimate profession, gathering the documentation required to obtain a residence permit is challenging. This uncertain grey zone, combined with stricter immigration policies and hostile rhetoric, has worsened the working conditions and safety of migrant sex workers in the UK. Many are reluctant to contact the police if they are subjected to violence and rape for fear of deportation.

In recent years, there has been a rise in the number of migrants, asylum seekers and refugees arriving in Europe, especially in and after 2015, due to conflicts and instability in countries like Syria, Iraq and Afghanistan. One study recorded some 49,000 irregular immigrants arrived in the UK in the year ending June 2025, 27 per cent more than the previous year.

Sometimes labelled a 'refugee crisis', many find it more accurate to label this increase as a political crisis about migration. This crisis is often referred to as a turning point, and it has definitely been turning point in the conversation about and focus on migration across Europe. In the UK, and elsewhere, an increase in migrants has spurred fear, and images of people arriving by boat – whether across the Mediterranean or the English Channel – have increased hostile rhetoric about migration. This fear and hostility often leads to simplistic and unsympathetic narratives, which are making migrants' status – and by extension, migrant sex workers' status – in the UK even more precarious.

I hope the stories shared in this book will help you to understand vulnerable migrant populations and people working in precarious conditions across borders, not only as people who need our understanding and support, but as individuals with agency, power and will.

Behind the statistics are ordinary human longing and care for families and loved ones. *Global Sex* is a story about the love mothers have for their children and how much they are willing to suffer for that love. It's about brutalities, bodies, feminism, capitalism, inequality and the difference privilege makes across borders in our global sharing of the present. It's about all of us.

Sine Plambech, Copenhagen, 2026

Beginner

Copenhagen, 2003

'Her breasts are average size.'

I'm looking at the woman in a lace bra, sitting across from me on the arm of a sofa.

'Hmm, OK. Thanks. I'll get back to you,' he answers.

The semi-naked woman shakes her head at me. 'You answered his question too honestly. Regardless of how we look in real life, on the phone we are always under thirty, with big breasts and long hair.' She is an experienced sex worker and I am an anthropologist, doing my first fieldwork at a brothel on the outskirts of Copenhagen. I am a new researcher in sex work. Over the past few months I have visited: a Thai man with a ponytail who sold sex to other men from his apartment; a Danish female sex worker who had dildos in several colours on a table covered in white velour and a round, red bed beneath a string of lights; and a Thai brothel in a damp basement in Copenhagen's red-light district, Istedgade, with a gold plastic cat waving in the window.

Now I have agreed to act as receptionist at the Danish brothel, where the woman with the average-sized breasts works. The sex workers I've been speaking to want me to try working here so I can gain insight into their world. They don't just want to be interviewed. They're testing how far I am willing to go to really understand their work. I have to speak with potential clients who call to ask about breast size, age, who is working and what kind of sex is offered on the brothel's laminated menu. I have to answer convincingly, so the clients will come in. But I'm a beginner at selling sex and I haven't yet understood the basic premise: sex is a commodity. And, as in any other transaction, you have to present the wares attractively.

I am sitting in the back room, trying to get clients to come into the brothel, while the women sit across from me, listening. Our roles have been marked out and reversed. They are the experts and my anthropological theories are no help to me. To lure in clients, all I have is my voice and my empathy.

We smoke cigarettes and chat. Two of the women are around forty, the third closer to fifty-five. One woman says, 'It's going to get busy soon.' It's lunchtime for the city's tradesmen. Before long, there is a knock on the brothel's basement door and I am asked to open it. A man is standing there in his work clothes. He says he's the one who called earlier. Evidently, I convinced him to come, despite the average-sized breasts. I let him in and he is shown to a room by one of the women. She closes the door behind them.

I return to the back room. A fourth woman enters. She is about fifty, thin, wearing a short skirt and a white lacy blouse. Having just finished a job with a client, she sits down on the sofa and takes a piece of chewing gum out of her bag. 'When you get wet down there, you get dry up here,' she says, popping the gum in her mouth. One of the women asks if I want to try having a customer. For real.

'No, thank you,' I say.

'But you can have one of the easy ones,' she says. 'We get men who would just want you to open your blouse while they're lying on the bed with one of us. It turns them on.' I shake my head.

We drink bitter coffee from a cafetiere and smoke more cigarettes. Our laughter is loud and raw. Two of the women here are cleaning assistants at a school, both single mothers who earn extra money at the brothel to make ends meet. They make 1,500 kroner[1] in one hour with a client. For seven hours of cleaning, they earn 500 kroner.[2]

On the way to the brothel, I cycled through Emdrup and down Søborg Hovedgade, where my grandmother Ella lives on a side street. I imagined she probably had no idea that there was a brothel right around the corner from her house. I thought of her again when a client came through the door. The men who come here are often tradesmen or retirees. They remind me of the men I have seen on the way home from the local market near my grandmother's, or of men walking with their little grandchildren on the way down to Utterslev Lake to feed the ducks. Here at the brothel, they are clients. Some of them want the women to lie down with them and hold them. They miss being touched. Several of them have sick wives who either don't want to have sex or can't. Others are widowers. Here, they are held and caressed, as long as they pay for it. After a few hours, they go back home.

'Our job is to make them feel special,' says one of the women. 'That's why we don't have a waiting room. We don't want the clients to see one another. This way, they

[1] 174 GBP (All currency conversions made in October 2025 and rounded to the nearest whole number.)
[2] 58 GBP

feel like they are paying for something that's not for other men. It's just for them and only them, something unique and genuine.' The clients and the women have an unspoken contract. They are buying and selling sex, care, caresses and passion. But it must feel authentic.

The Notebooks

I wrote about this brothel in one of my first anthropological notebooks. For twenty years since then, I have been writing field notes from various places around the world. Back then, at the brothel on the outskirts of Copenhagen, only Danish women worked there. Today, many of Denmark's sex workers – as in the rest of the world – are migrant women. They cross national borders to sell sex on the other side of the globe. I have followed the trail of sex work from windblown brothels in Thy, on Denmark's west coast, to raids in the red-light district of Vesterbro by Copenhagen police. I have done fieldwork among sex workers in Pattaya and Bangkok in Thailand, and Nigeria and Dubai. I have worked with female migrants who travelled by boat to sell sex in Libya and Sicily. I have heard their stories of dangerous journeys across the Sahara Desert and the Mediterranean, in the hope of a better life in Europe. I have notes from long periods in steamy towns in Thailand and in crowded, dusty districts in Lagos and Benin City, Nigeria. The fieldwork has been constant, because the women are now online. Almost every day, I have contact with them and hear about their situations through WhatsApp, Facebook Messenger or phone calls. Everything from their travel plans, questions about the best routes to Europe, selfies with pouty lips, photos of newborn babies and pictures of what they're eating. My notebooks through the years are filled with their stories.

A stack of the author's anthropological notebooks

Now I have reopened the notebooks. On each empty first page inside the cover, the factory has printed IN CASE OF LOSS, PLEASE RETURN TO____ and I had written my name and mobile number there. On the next line, it reads AS A REWARD: $__, but I never wrote an amount on the blank line. I can't put a value on my notebooks. They are unique and irreplaceable. The thought of giving a reward feels irrelevant and unimaginable. They are never in an attic where I could not reach them if there were a fire, never in a cellar that could flood. They are in a safe place. They are part of me, and I guard them as anyone would guard their most precious belongings.

I am rereading my notebooks at a point in my life when I am restless; seeking something. My mother died suddenly and unexpectedly just a few days after I gave birth to my daughter, Ella – my third child and the first in my newly constructed family. I need to pause and take some time. I feel a longing to reflect amid the chaos of death, life, motherhood, family and my intense work as an anthropologist in vulnerable communities. My notebooks are my witnesses. They are worn, handwritten; with long, detailed descriptions, random thoughts and questions that sprung from conversations, interviews, data and from the unspoken, which arises somewhere between the words someone has said to me, what I wrote down and how I wrote it. The notebooks contain all the wisdom I have collected in my work. It feels as if there is something in these books that I have to find and understand.

I open the books with a different, more inquisitive attitude and I discover details, reminders and notes in the margins which I had overlooked before. These are notes about my own life, invisible, uneasy, messy, incomplete, private and personal matters, side by side with the women's lives. These notes are unavoidably present; I can't ignore them. I never thought before that my own experiences were relevant to understanding my research, but there is no way around these insistent notes, their unfiltered revelations about my life and my choices. They tell a story about me, as a woman alongside and together with the women central to my work. And they tell a larger, global and political story of love, colonialism and capitalism. A story about the difference it makes where we are born.

Writing this Book

'I like that the book is about my life,' says Lom. 'I would like my children to know, one day, how I provided for them.' I had asked her if she thought it was OK if I wrote a book telling her story and I was touched by her answer. Not just because she would participate in the book, but because she felt it was important that her children learn her story someday. I know how hard it is for some of the women to tell their children how they provided for them when they were little.

Lom, from Thailand, is one of the women in this book. I also write about Sommai, Becky and Vivian. I have met and written about more than a hundred women in my notebooks over the years, but these four have special meaning for me. These are the women I have asked about everything that is difficult, vulnerable and important, zigzagging between the intimate and the global. Their life histories are unique, but also have much in common with other women I have met. All of them, despite the many times life has ambushed them, dispel the myth of migrant sex workers as nothing more than passive victims of coercion, trafficking, violence, patriarchy and poverty. Instead, they see themselves almost as rebels, problem-solvers and hard workers, who would not be satisfied with poverty, unemployment and a rough life for themselves, their children and their families.

Sommai, Lom, Becky and Vivian are not made anonymous.[i] They want me to tell their stories and they know – as do I – that they would not do it themselves. For even though they can read and write fairly well, and went to school until between Year 5 and Year 8, they prefer to send voice notes and emojis, or call on the phone instead of writing. When they have a complicated document about residency, legal or medical issues, they have someone else read it aloud for them. Most of all, they are busy living their lives, working, raising their children, not writing their life stories.

But is the fact that they can't, don't have time, can't afford to, or that they are helping others, a good enough reason for me to tell their stories? Shouldn't sex workers and migrants write their own stories? Since I am white, not a migrant, not a sex worker, should I do this?

I have known the women I am writing about for many years, through births, deaths, travels, illness and laughter. But there will always be a power imbalance between us. It doesn't disappear, even though these women want me to tell their stories. I am the one, not them, sitting at the desk, writing this book, with a salary, a computer, an editor, a PhD and a free, state-sponsored education behind me. What makes me different from them is that I have my Danish passport, my citizenship, my social safety net, my white skin. I can cross borders without issue. Because of my work, I become close with women who live and work in unsafe places. But they live there all the time, while I can leave and return to the safety of my home.

There are no clear answers to these questions. But I have tried, in close collaboration with the women themselves, to describe their lives and the complex global context within which they exist. They watched me write in my notebooks every time we were together.

The notes are rewritten into condensed stories with their guidance. I have read the texts aloud to them, so they could approve them, make suggestions and comments. They have refined the details of descriptions of events and experiences, helped to find words and precise place names, approved photographs, and told me if they agree with the way I describe them, the way I have analysed and tried to approach an understanding of their lives.

Anthropology is a scientific, but also a colonial, project. The position of the anthropologist or the researcher relative to the people being researched has been debated, with good reason. But it doesn't seem enough anymore simply to disclose one's own identity, position of power, and whatever privileges a person has that shape the blind spots in their research, and then just keep writing.

I decided to write these women's raw and honest stories with the obligation that I also disclose what I find in the notebooks about my own life – messiness, therapy, vulnerability, privileges and where they come from. When I tell their candid, private stories, it demands my courage to relinquish the image of the polished, distanced researcher, who simply observes 'the other', without getting personally involved.

I think we need to be more exposed. I think we have to go deeper, messier, braver, more honestly and with more solidarity. We have to be willing to try, to make mistakes and to explore different approaches, take personal risks. From the more intimate topics like parenting, loss, grief, love and debt, to how we are connected to colonialism, slavery and exploitation. To be open to fragility and shame, which are essential to our empathy, our compassion and our interpretation.

I have felt hesitant about involving myself and I know that I risk, on the one hand, being considered unscientific, and on the other hand, being questioned for taking up space, as a white person. But it has to be this way. I will write the story of these women and where it is relevant, I will bring in my own experiences to highlight theirs. The fact that I expose parts of my own life does not remove the asymmetry between them and me, even though my intent is solidarity. At times, my notebooks dissolve the barrier between 'the researcher' and 'the researched', between myself and them. But world history flows painfully and constantly between us.

Follow the Money

Where there is money, there will be sex.

My notes and my research follow sex on a journey across the globe. But my work is also a journey in the footprints of global capitalism. I have followed along, too, as the women I am researching gradually began travelling to new places, because it was too difficult, expensive or dangerous to make it to Europe and because there was money to be made elsewhere.

Sommai, Lom, Becky and Vivian left their homelands – Thailand and Nigeria – to work in South Korea, Malaysia, Denmark, Italy, England, Libya and Dubai. They chose their destinations according to where there was money to be earned and, sometimes, contingent on where the borders were more open. They were not influenced by whether it was legal or not to be a sex worker, but instead, where there were opportunities. Where they had access.

I have tracked the global sex worker marketplace, but especially women from Thailand and Nigeria. Women from these lands make up two of the largest groups of sex workers in Denmark, and throughout Europe.[ii] Typically, they come from two regions: the Thai women come from Isaan in north-east of their country and the Nigerian women come from Benin City, in southern Edo State. It may be more accurate to say that the women have followed in the footsteps of the men who have followed in the footsteps of global capitalism and sometimes in the footsteps of war. The first sex tourists in Pattaya, Thailand, were white, Western European men and American soldiers on 'rest and recreation' from the Vietnam War. Later, soldiers followed from the wars in Iraq and Afghanistan, with American soldiers in particular going to Pattaya.

During the 1990s, travel to Thailand became more accessible to European men. For instance, Larsen Travel Agency arranged charter tours from Denmark to Thailand for 4,999 kroner,[3] which was an affordable price for men who worked in factories, who were without degrees or in low-paying jobs. For women from the rural regions of impoverished Isaan, it became possible to earn good money in the tourist areas and more and more women moved there, some with hopes of marrying a client and migrating to the West.

When the Russian, Middle Eastern and Chinese economies also started to grow in the 1990s, new groups of men could afford to travel to exotic places to buy sex. There was a new market and new demand. Russian and Nigerian women became a growing group among sex workers in places like Pattaya. The booming construction industries in Malaysia, South Korea, Singapore and the United Arab Emirates needed male migrant workers and the sex workers followed them. Not high-end escorts, but women who sold sex at massage parlours, which the migrant men could afford. As new capitalist centres grew, businessmen travelled there without their families, to invest, hold meetings and develop new projects. And in the hotel bars, sex workers appeared. They migrated from their villages across borders, and also within their own countries, to work in sex tourism near exotic beaches. Some

[3] Approximately 580 GBP in the mid-1990s.

Nigerian women migrated from the poor, Islamic north to the slightly wealthier, Christian south of Nigeria and, from there, onwards to Europe. The goal was the same: to earn money and thereby potentially change their lives and the lives of their children and families.

'We have to seek politics in invisible places,' wrote anthropologist Charles Piot in 2010.[iii] Sex work is one of these invisible places. 'The political' is found not only in well-known places, powerful and grand, but also in intimacy, the body and relations – places where we don't necessarily look for it. The purchase and sale of sex reflects new emerging economies, gender politics, inequality, global migration policy, old and new privileges. Who is selling sex, who is buying it, why and where? And where does the money that sex workers earn get sent and why? What is it used for?

To follow the money, the transactions, the people, and see what that reveals about capitalism, about colonialism, desire and longing, is not a new phenomenon. Anthropologist Sidney Mintz wrote in 1985 about the historical journey of sugar, from the European tropical colonies as a 'slave crop', to an elite luxury item and then a common food for the working class in Europe, to today's modern and excessively sweetened diet. Through sugar, Mintz showed the evolution of industrial capitalism.[iv] Journalist Naomi Klein viewed the world through corporate logos in her book of capitalist critque *No Logo*, in 1999.[v] By following the history of the production of brands such as Nike and Pepsi and their supply chains from factories in the global south, where many of the world's poorer countries are located, to consumers in wealthier countries, many in the global north, she showed the invasive economic forces and destructive social effects in the wake of globalised commercialism. Similarly, the Italian journalist Roberto Saviano, in his 2015 book *Zero Zero Zero* observed the world through the journey of cocaine, from Colombia to Mexico and on to Europe.[vi] Through the white powder, we see how criminality, politics and global economics are interwoven with people's need for intoxication and self-medication.

By following the trail of sugar, commercial brands and cocaine, Mintz, Klein and Saviano map out the invisible relationships between human desire and global dynamics. Intoxication, escapism and pleasure connect the human body to dizzying global forces through a snort of white powder up the nose, the sweetness of sugar on the tongue or a cool new pair of trainers.

Sex work is a prism in a similar way, reflecting the changing world and following the routes of global capitalism. Sex and sex work are a distillation of what is global and local, down to the most intimate stage: the bed.

What Is a Dane Doing Here?

Thy, 2003

'What is a Dane doing here?' an older woman with a Thai-Thy accent asks sternly, while looking up at me quickly from her playing cards. She is sitting on the floor with a group of Thai women. All of them have cards in their hands and bowls of food in front of them, emitting the intense aroma of fish sauce and chilli peppers. 'Sine is OK,' my Thai friend reassures her. 'She is from Jylland too.' The woman looks back down at her cards. This is my first time meeting Sommai.

My friend had picked me up in her metallic-brown VW Golf at the bus stop on the main road. She was living with her Thai mother and Danish father in a small red single-family home, with pink orchids in the window and a view of the neighbours' pig barn. She had entered first and taken off her shoes. I followed her and did the same. In the kitchen on a red countertop, coriander leaves, vegetables and pieces of washed chicken lay draining in a colander. The rice cooker made the kitchen warm and steamy. I could already hear the women's laughing and shouting from the card game. The house felt alive.

I had just begun my fieldwork with Thai women in Thy, a region in the north-west corner of Jylland, Denmark. I was renting a straw-thatched old farmhouse on the island of Mors and I did not have a driver's licence. So I took the local blue bus to the main street and, from there, the women would drive me to the small villages where the bus did not go. It was November and I was seven months pregnant with my second child, Carl. My plan was to finish my fieldwork before I gave birth. I sat on the bus with my pregnant belly and looked out at the landscape. The bus drove past soft contours of brown ploughed fields, barely moving windmills, the biscuit factory and 'The Mussel', where mussels from the Limfjord are cleaned and packaged by Thai and Polish women. A woman of Asian heritage in a big coat waves the bus to a stop every morning. Behind her lies a pig farm, where she lives or works perhaps. The bus driver knows her and they exchange a few congenial words which I cannot hear.

Sometimes I wait inside the bus stop at Nykøbing Mors, which is a hub for getting anywhere. One day, two men were waiting there in heavy, dark-blue overalls. Two rifles were sticking out of one of their sports bags. They asked me which bus I was waiting for and if I was visiting family. 'I'm going to visit my friend from Thailand,' I said.

One responded, 'Yeah, there are a lot of them here,' staring down at the tarmac.

We stood in silence for a while. I couldn't quite figure them out, but then the one with the bag said, 'But that's good, because we need women here. When they come from the outside, it keeps us from inbreeding.' He smiled at me conspiratorially.

'That's what some people say,' I replied. 'I read in an old article that some people think there was inbreeding on Mors in the old days, because the families intermarried.' The men laughed and then it was quiet again. They eyed me with suspicion and I wondered if perhaps I had said too much. Then the man with the bag said mischievously, 'Sure, sure, but it's much worse over in Salling.' They both nodded towards the other side of the fjord.

I know Salling, Mors, Thy and central Jylland. I come from here, just like the accents of the women, their husbands, their new in-laws, their co-workers, their boyfriends and their clients at the massage parlour do. My central Jylland background gives me a ticket of entry to their Thai-Jylland world and I am admitted as one of their own, a local. Though I am always Danish, and not Thai.

To the sound of Sommai and the other women gambling in the next room, that evening I learn to play 'children's' card games. Not for money. 'We all come from the same village in Thailand,' says my friend over her hand of cards. She continues, with a sense of near-reverence, 'Sommai, who you met, was one of the first Thai women in Thy.'

On the sofa in the room with us sit three Danish men. They don't say much. One is Niels, an accountant who is married to Sommai. My friend says, with a laugh, 'They're here because they're nervous that their wives are risking too much of their families' money.'

At the end of the evening, I get the phone numbers of the women playing cards, including Sommai's. I call her the next day and explain in detail why I would like to meet her again.

One morning, a couple of days later, she picks me up in her car at Thisted Station. I am nervous about meeting her again, after her stern greeting, but in the driver's seat next to me sits an intelligent, warm and affable woman. 'It was embarrassing that you saw us playing for money,' she says, laughing. 'We didn't know if you were going to tell the police.' We drive to her and

Niels' house on a quiet residential street abutting a field on the outskirts of Thisted. Homemade Thai food is ready on the counter under aluminum foil. I stay all day; we talk and eat. I ask her questions carefully and she slowly opens up about her life story.

Sommai

'Dear Dad, I have left for Pattaya. I am asking your permission to do something about our life, because I can't take it any more. Take good care of the kids.'

Sitting in her living room in Thy, Sommai says, 'That was what I wrote in the note to my father when I left in 1990. I took my in-laws' radio, left their house with my four children and boarded the bus to the big city, Khorat. When I got there, I pawned the radio and used the money for a bus ticket to Pattaya. The few coins I had left I divided between my children, so they could take the bus back without me to my parents' house. I folded the note for my father and put it in my eldest daughter's shirt pocket. After the kids left, I got on my bus.'

Sommai knew that she would be working at a bar in Pattaya, selling sex to clients. But her plan was to find a foreigner, a farang, so she could leave the country and find a job. At the time, she was living with her children at her in-laws' house. Her husband was working in Saudi Arabia, but he didn't send much money back home. And it did not go far, when she had to provide for her children, her in-laws, her own parents, her terminally ill sister and her sister's six children. As a day labourer, she tended oxen, standing in water up to her knees every morning. Her feet were swollen and covered in insect bites. Once, she had to humiliatingly ask to borrow five kilos of rice from the richest woman in their village, the landowner, Pen.

'Without money,' explains Sommai, 'you are invisible, like air, you're nothing.'

A few months before Sommai wrote the note to her father, she had met a Thai woman who was married to an American man. The woman owned a bar in Pattaya and she was attending the wedding of a woman from her bar, which was taking place near Sommai's village.

'Why are you slaving away here?' she asked Sommai. 'You are still pretty. You can work at my bar if you want.' At first, Sommai said no, but in the end, she didn't see another way out. She wrote the note to her father and left.

The bar had a red facade and Sommai remembers it as a cosy place with a lot of people and a vibrant atmosphere. She was shown to an area with a tile floor on the second level, above the bar, where the women shared a large private room and a bathroom. After a night's work in the bar, the ones who were not with clients at hotel rooms rolled out their sleeping mats.

Pattaya was throbbing music, flirting and partying every single night. Sommai had just arrived from the country; she was thirty-three years old, which was getting on in years for a 'bar girl', as she called herself. She would have to appear young here to attract clients. She was wearing her worn clothing from the village, but the younger women gave her some of theirs so she would fit in. She wore tight skirts and low-cut blouses, which she would never have dreamt of wearing to a party back home. She was drunk every night at the start, because she was supposed to drink with the clients. Later, she learned from the other women to dump her drinks out into the plastic bucket under the bar when the clients weren't looking. When a man entered the bar alone, Sommai would walk over to him. Some of the men were sweet and shy. They didn't know how to ask Sommai to come back to their hotel rooms. Others were more experienced and asked without hesitation about the price and how many hours or minutes and what she was willing to do.

'The first time I was with a client,' she says, 'I tried to hide my face. I felt that I was so bad at this work. It was hard to be with clients and to have strangers touching me after so many years with my husband. I had never been unfaithful to him, had never been naked in front of anyone but him. And when he and I had sex, it was under a blanket or in the dark behind a curtain. I never walked around naked at home or got up naked from the bed, because we always lived with so many people and we never had a bedroom with a locked door . . .

'I met a Scottish man. He was blond and young and very different from anyone I had ever met before. Even though he paid me, being with him reminded me of a boyfriend I had before I got married. He was a young man from my village and I was very much in love with him. With the Scottish man, sex was different. I had had sex with my husband for the sake of having children, because he was mostly interested in himself. But the Scottish man wasn't like that. We travelled around Thailand for three weeks. He tried to get a visa for me, so I could go back with him. I was already imagining my new life in Scotland. But the visa was denied. I think of him sometimes,' she says, with a wistful look.

A visa is a fateful document which can change everything: men, countries, sex and a person's future.

Take Me With You

One evening, the mama-san came to get Sommai in the common room above the bar. She wasn't supposed to be working, but all the other women were busy with clients, so she had to go down. Niels from Thy was sitting at the bar. Sommai went over and sat next to him. She had learned a bit of English and Niels knew some too. At first, Niels wasn't interested in taking Sommai back to his hotel room. He had been with another woman the night before. But Sommai was persistent and said that she would pay him to take her with him. He laughed and paid.

Sommai and Niels talked about their families. Niels was divorced and had been living alone with his daughter for eight years. As they chatted and joked, they felt that they understood one another. Something clicked between them. They were together for ten days and then Niels had to return home. He missed her. He called and asked if she would like to try coming to Denmark. He would pay for her ticket and if it didn't work out, she could go back. She agreed and he sent her a ticket to fly with Aeroflot via Moscow.

When Sommai and Niels drove in the car from the airport across Aggersund Bridge for the first time, Thy's flat landscape, the sky and fields reminded Sommai of Isaan. And the quiet. She enjoyed this return to the country, away from noisy Pattaya. For the next three months, Niels and Sommai built on their meeting in Pattaya. They talked and Niels showed

Sommai and Niels on the beach in Pattaya in the days following their meeting at the bar

Sommai around Thy. Sommai's visa ran out and she returned home, but the next year she came back with her youngest son, six-year-old Pila, and married Niels at Thisted City Hall.

In the wedding picture, Niels is wearing a grey suit. He has on glasses with thick black frames and Sommai is wearing a brown dress with her hair teased up high with small barrettes. They look happy and a bit nervous. But there is also something proud and defiant about the picture.

'There were no guests,' says Sommai one day when I'm visiting, and we're talking in the kitchen about their wedding and her first time living in Denmark. 'And no bridal bouquet. I'm still mad at you about that, Niels,' she says, laughing. 'I didn't know that Danish women got bouquets.'

Pila told me later about the day his mother left. 'My siblings and I went with my mother to the city. She was holding a radio. I didn't know what she was going to do with it. Later, I found out that she sold it to get money for her ticket to Pattaya. She gave us each some money before she put us on a bus to our grandparents' house. I bought a lottery ticket and won fifty baht.[4] That was a lot of money back then. I kept it in my pocket, because I was waiting to tell my mother and give her the money. But she never came. One day, someone told me that she had gone to Pattaya. Finally, I gave the money to my grandmother. Then I learned that my mother had flown to a country called Denmark. Whenever I saw a plane in the sky, I thought it was her coming back home to me. And whenever the bus from Bangkok stopped

[4] 1 GBP

on the main street near our house, I looked to see if my mother would get out. But it was never her. Many months later, she came back and brought me with her to Denmark.'

I repeated Pila's story to Sommai. She reached for a paper towel on the counter and dried her tears.

I'm Sending You Home

Thy, 2023

I call Sommai on FaceTime, because even though I have written detailed notes and have heard her speak about her first trip to Denmark many times, I am still missing a few details. She is sitting, like so many times before, in her kitchen in Thy. It is a warm summer day and she is drinking juice after dropping off two old kitchen cabinets at the landfill. Niels is puttering around shirtless behind her. She is talking while I revise my text.

'When I arrived at the airport in Moscow, all the signs were in Russian, so I followed some people I thought looked Danish. I didn't need a visa to visit Denmark, just my letter of invitation from Niels. He was an accountant, so I thought he had it all figured out. We thought so. At customs in Copenhagen, the officer in the airport asked for my passport and my return ticket. I pulled them from my plastic bag. He looked at me and asked, "What is the reason for your visit?"

'"I'm on vacation," I said.

'"For how long?"

'"I don't know." That's when it started to go badly. I didn't know much English.

'"Do you have any money?"

'"No, I am visiting my boyfriend."

'"What is his name?"

I couldn't pronounce his name. "I have it here in my pocketbook."

'"You need money to come in. If you have no money, I will send you back on the same plane you arrived on." He pointed in the direction of the planes. "I am sending you home," he repeated. "Sit on the bench and wait there."

'So I waited, for two hours, Sine. I was terrified. I didn't know if I was going to jail. In Thailand, we are afraid of the police. They put you in jail. I had never been arrested before and this felt like I was being arrested. I was mostly afraid because I hadn't told anyone that I had left for Denmark. Not my mother or father, not my children. I didn't want anyone to know about it, in case it didn't go well with Niels, in case I wasn't able to get away from Pattaya. I wanted it to work out for the sake of my family and I didn't want to lose face in my village. But if I were put in jail, then no one would know where I was. I wasn't afraid of dying, but I was afraid of disappearing and that my parents and my children would not be able to find out what happened. That they wouldn't be able to find me.'

Sommai tears off a piece of paper towel, takes off her glasses and dries her eyes. 'I don't know why I'm crying,' she says. 'But it was one of the worst days of my life. It was one of the worst experiences I ever had ... I was sitting there on the bench, poor, not knowing anyone, not knowing anything and without anyone knowing who I was. And in front of me was a policeman who felt hostile.'

The police detained her for several hours at the airport customs office. Niels had said that he would meet her at the exit. But there were no mobile phones back then, so she couldn't contact him and ask if he was there, or explain to him what happened. She was afraid that Niels wouldn't be in the arrivals hall when the police went looking for him. Maybe he had been waiting and had given up when she didn't come out after such a long time. Maybe he thought that she had tricked him, because she knew he had been nervous about that. That was why he had sent her a ticket and not just the money to buy one. If he had left and gone back home, all was lost.

'I tried to explain to the policeman that I was afraid my boyfriend would leave. He just said, "If he really came to pick you up, then he will wait." I noticed another Thai woman who had been on the same flight as me. She was allowed to proceed to the arrivals hall. I said that if she saw a stooped man, to tell him that I had been detained. She found Niels.'

Now Niels interrupts her. 'So I went to the Aeroflot office. But they said that everyone from the Thailand plane had been let through. They wouldn't tell me about anyone who had been detained, or what happened.'

After checking all the paperwork, the police decided to call Niels over the loudspeaker. 'We are seeking Niels Molbæk,' they announced. Niels found the office. 'Do you know her?' asked the policeman, pointing at Sommai. 'What is her name and how old is she?'

'I was able to remember that from the ticket I had sent,' said Niels. 'They asked if we were planning to get married. I said, "Yes, I hope so." I had to guarantee them that I would provide for her and that I would send her home if we did not get married within three months. So they gave me her return ticket and wrote, "Cannot be changed". Finally, we were allowed to leave, but when we turned to go, the officer said, "You are not free yet. We are going to call Thisted Police and check on you."' Niels takes a rare, long look into the phone camera. 'That was humbling. It was as if they were enjoying it.'

Thai Lady Seeks Husband

For several years, Sommai swung her feet out of the double bed at 4 a.m. every morning, got ready for the day and then started up her green moped, which Niels had bought for her. 'The kind that doesn't go more than 30 kilometres an hour,' she says, 'which I could drive without a moped licence. I sped off in cold and darkness to Kvickly supermarket to clean until nine, seven days a week. I attended the Thisted Language School and had four cleaning jobs, because I took all the jobs they would give me. I drove around Thy on my Puch Maxi. If the boss of the cleaning company asked if anybody wanted a cleaning job on the Oslo Ferry, I volunteered for that too. I worked constantly. Sometimes Niels said that I should be home more and with my children, but my family had been poor for so long and it seemed like I was earning so much money at work. The four cleaning jobs were easier than tending oxen in the village or being with clients in Pattaya. I made about 11,000 kroner[5] per month in Denmark, while in Pattaya I only made about 1,000 kroner.[6] From my wages in Denmark, I was able to send 2,000–3,000 kroner[7] home to Thailand each month. That was a lot of money. But there were also a lot of hospital bills at that time. When my mother, my father and my sister

[5] 1277 GBP
[6] 116 GBP
[7] 235–348 GBP

died, there were fewer people back home who needed the money, so I sent less.'

'How did it feel,' I ask, 'to suddenly have money?'

'I remember feeling proud of myself. I had never seen so much money at one time in Thailand. And I didn't think it was that hard. I was used to working hard and helping my family. I had always done that. In Pattaya, you couldn't say no. You had to go with the men who wanted you and you worked seven nights a week, all night. If I didn't go with the men, I only got base wages from the bar, about 350 kroner.[8] And the men decided what I would do with them in the hotel. But in my cleaning jobs, it was just me; no one else, only me. And I could turn down jobs if I wanted.'

Later, Sommai got a driver's licence, a small car and a steady job at a metals factory. She sat in blue overalls at her machine and pressed out little metal pieces at a speed that no one else in the factory could match.

I visited Sommai at her job and eventually talked to her co-workers too. She was well liked. She was fast and efficient and when she was at work, things happened. She arranged Thai cultural evenings where she made food for her co-workers and they were especially well attended by men. Sometimes she had photos of women from Thailand who were dreaming about finding a Danish man. The photos had been enhanced to lighten and smooth the women's skin, to make them seem paler and younger. Her close co-worker came to one of these evenings and later married a Thai woman named Sit. 'I saw a photo of her,' he said. 'I can't say it was love at first sight, but I thought she was pretty.'

In time, Sommai found several Danish men for poor

[8] 41 GBP

Sommai at the metal factory in Thy

women from her family and her circles in Isaan. Some women were widows; some had husbands who drank, or hit them, or had debts; some women sold sex, but wanted to do something else. Niels helped with the paperwork, but they never took any money for it. 'It was to help people who were just like me,' says Sommai. The men were sometimes her co-workers at the factory, but more often they were someone who knew someone who knew someone who was interested in having a Thai wife. Other times, they put advertisements in the local papers with the heading, 'Thai lady seeks husband'.

Eventually, the Thai women and their husbands created a community in Thy and many more have arrived since then. Back when Sommai and Niels got married, in 1992, there were only two Thai women in Thy. In 2023, there are nearly a thousand. Some were sex workers before they came. Some are sex workers now. Most of them have had, or have, other kinds of work. But together the Thai women of Thy created a small community with card games, birthday parties, crabbing, mushroom hunting and their own Buddhist temple. As children, they caught frogs in the rice paddies, picked fruit, grew coriander and chilli peppers – the common plants in Isaan, the area most of them came from. Now they were learning about a new landscape. Mussels from the Limfjord were preserved in large Mason jars. They picked mushrooms and caught crabs with bits of meat stuffed into a nylon stocking. They sowed coriander, chilli peppers and cucumbers in their Danish husbands' often-unused greenhouses and saved seeds for the next year. Nothing was wasted. In time, Sommai brought her youngest daughter over to Denmark. Her eldest son had to remain in Thailand and her eldest daughter went to Pattaya, met a man, and moved to Switzerland.

The Menu

Thy, 2006

Sommai and I drive to the local Thai massage parlour – she knows the women who work there. The gravel crunches under our feet in the parking area behind the building, where the cars can be parked, hidden from the main road. A Thai woman is standing in the doorway. 'I saw you on the camera,' she says, waving lovingly at Sommai. I notice two wooden clubs behind the entry door. The woman who opened the door follows my gaze. 'That's to protect myself,' she says.

We sit on her bed. Around her are Buddha figurines, a make-up table and blinking strings of lights on the ceiling. A television plays news from Thailand in the corner. There have been floods for several days in southern Thailand and soldiers are stacking sandbags to keep the water away from the houses and people. She says that she sent a donation to help the victims. She coughs lightly and says that she's feeling sick. Even though the parlour is open twenty-four hours a day, she is too tired to see clients today. Sommai has brought her food and painkillers.

The woman lives here and works here. The house is laid out like the brothel in Copenhagen where I worked as receptionist. While we chat, I hear cars speeding by on the busy road outside.

A door opens to a little white hot tub, where the clients can bathe. At most massage parlours, the clients are asked to wash before sex. There are two other rooms in the house, but the other women are not here today.

I have met this woman before, so she knows that I want to know more about her work and her life. She trusts me because I am with Sommai. 'I tell my family in Thailand that I work as a cleaner in Denmark and that is why I can send home 18,000 baht[9] each month.' Sommai makes a calculation and says, 'What you are sending equals about three months' wages in Thailand.'

The woman continues, 'I had a job at the fish factory, but you have to wake up so early and drive alone in the dark to work. It's hard work and doesn't pay well. This job is hard too, but I get much more money for my family. There are clients who shout, who smell, who are drunk, and one of the clients tried to rape me in the tub. I got him off me and threw him out. We have become better at only allowing proper clients in. We check the camera and watch out for each other. We don't allow just anyone in and we make them wash first, and we use condoms, and I generally only do it with my regulars. It's harder for the women who are new. They have to hurry up and earn as much as they can. We have a lot of clients from Poland right now. They live in the houses out here and work on the farms.'

We eat and then watch more TV from Thailand. Sommai and the woman talk about their common friends and their families in Thailand. They agree to collect more money to send to the flood area.

When we drive away, Sommai says, 'A few months ago, I had to defend her. There was a Christmas party

[9] 414 GBP

at the factory and we played Christmas bingo. Everyone was supposed to bring a gift and my co-worker, Ole, brought a menu from the massage parlour as his gift. He mowed the lawn at the parlour sometimes and maybe he was a client too. I don't know. But he took one of their menus and hung it on the wall where all the gifts were hung with red ribbons.

'I asked Ole to take the menu down, but he wouldn't, saying that it was just for fun. I got angry. "Do you think the woman at the parlour would think it's a fun gift? She is not working out there for fun." I told a co-worker, who told our boss, and the menu was taken down.

'I drank cola all night, but people got drunk and Ole kept saying obscene things to me. Later, when people were leaving to go into town, he suggested that we go over to the massage parlour. I was so furious and embarrassed. "Why are you making fun of us?" I yelled. "I am the only Thai here."

'"It was just for fun," he said.

'I yelled and cried at the same time, "Maybe it's fun for you, but it is not fun for me. It is not fun for us. And if you don't stop, I will throw my drink at you." My manager came up behind me and held me and calmed me down. He told Ole to stop. I put on my coat and drove home.'

'I remember you told me that story before,' I said. 'But the way I remember it you actually did throw your cola on him before leaving.'

She laughed. 'You're thinking of the time I poured coffee on my other co-worker the day I was in the canteen. He was sitting across from me while I ate my food. He said that his friend had just been in Thailand and that he said you just "put 100 kroner on the bar and you can screw all night".

'"Your friend said that?" I asked. "I don't believe it. That's not true, you can't pay 100 kroner for a whole night." My co-worker didn't know that I had worked in Pattaya myself.

'"Well, I believe it," he said. A couple of the other men said, "I wish that was me. We should take a trip to Thailand," and they laughed.

'I said, "Don't laugh at us. Keep it up and I'll throw my coffee at you." But he didn't stop. So I took my plastic mug and dumped it out on him. It was only luke warm. I was so angry. Five of my female co-workers came and told him to apologise to me, and he did.'

'You dump drinks on men who provoke you,' I say.

She looks at me and we start laughing. 'I do, when I feel like I can't do anything else.'

Anthro-Kids

In 2003, a few months after my first fieldwork in Thy, Carl was born. I wrote my project about the Thai women in Thy while my foot rocked his red bouncy chair in our apartment in Copenhagen. My husband Morten and I had an eight-year-old son, Julius, as well. I didn't know it yet, but Thy would be the beginning of a life of research, fieldwork and children. Since then, I have had two more children and am a mother of four. They have all accompanied me on my fieldwork, both inside and outside of my womb.

Before I went to Thy for the first time, I read in a report from the National Association of Danish Women's Crisis Centres that they did not know why Thai women 'burned all their bridges behind them in Thailand' and moved to Denmark.[vii] There was a lot of speculation that these women were passive, being bought and utilised to service sex-fixated Danish men. But here in my first project, I had to conclude that I had not met women who had burned their bridges. I had met women who had lots of good reasons to be in Denmark – some of them had good lives, others had really difficult lives, lives with violence, too. But none of them had travelled to burn their bridges or to disown their families in Thailand. On the contrary, they left to try to support their families and to provide for their children, whom they often had to leave behind with family members. Some of them got married, some were sex workers. But all of the women

I had met in Thy sent money home – and the sex workers sent the most.

The women in Thy speak of Thailand as their home. They speak about their families and the children there. They miss them, they call them, they watch Thai television. They sit on the floor in warm fleece tops, in front of the wood stove, eating Thai food. Thy was connected to Thailand, and I knew I would have to travel there to see where the women came from. I had never been before and I was going with Morten and our two boys. We were not going as tourists, but to follow the journey of the women, to Isaan, to live in Sommai's village for three months. I took Thai language classes and learned a few simple sentences: 'What is your name?' 'What do you do?' 'May I come and speak with your family?'

Julius was ten and Carl was two. We put Carl in a baby backpack and packed one extra backpack. I brought two blank notebooks.

The author with her son, Carl, on the train to north-east Thailand in 2005

Nintendo

Mo Baan, 2006

It is dark when we arrive on the train from Bangkok and are met by Chai in his pickup truck. We sit in the bed of the truck while he drives us further and further into the country. In the beams from the headlights, I can make out red dirt, rice paddies and villages, while the rainbow-coloured double-decker buses from Bangkok pass us, honking. The road is not paved for the last half hour and Chai navigates carefully around the muddy potholes in the road on the way to his house.

Large insects are flapping around a bulb in the ceiling of the porch entry. It is April, the hottest month in Thailand. We are staying with Chai and Bun in one of the newly built migrant homes in the village. We are given a room where we fall asleep together on a mattress on the floor, with the breeze from a little electric fan flowing over us.

The next morning, heat hovers over the village. It smells of smoke, from the small fires where women are boiling water and roasting fish. A repetitive scratchy voice is being broadcast from a speaker at the temple. My boys are sweltering. It is too hot to play outside and there is nothing to do within the stifling, empty house. Bun and Chai have gone to the market. I fill a big basin with cold water and put both my boys inside. I feel guilty about my family. We are far from any doctors or hospitals and I am suddenly filled with panic over what would happen if one of the kids got sick or got hurt out here. Julius is trying to make contact with the Thai children in front of the house. They are racing around on bicycles without seats, while buses and trucks speed by them on the road. He comes back without success. They threw water at him. I have to do something, fast.

When Chai returns, I ask if he will drive us to the larger city nearby, even though he just picked us up from there the day before. We pay for the petrol and, when we get there, purchase a little Nintendo for Julius. The other children don't have one. I feel like I'm both a bad mother and a bad anthropologist. My son seems completely demolished by village life on the first day and it feels wrong to use our money this way. I feel split down the middle between my work and my family. But the Nintendo attracts other children. They gather around Julius and wait wide-eyed for a chance to try the game. They play too, and slowly we become a part of life in the village.

Two Women on a Scooter

An older woman with thick glasses cooks noodle soup in large, dented pots every day, out by the village's only intersection. This is the village centre, with a school, a phone box, a grocer and a temple, each on one of the corners. People on their way home from work in the fields buy hot, spicy soup in plastic bags, sprinkle chilli flakes and sugar on top, and drive home on their scooters. This is the village takeaway, but also a meeting place where I sit with the boys, drink cola, slurp soup and chat with people. I quickly realise that even though I learned a bit of Thai before starting my fieldwork, I need an interpreter. The noodle woman contacts Ying for me, because she knows that she speaks English.

Ying, in her eighth month of pregnancy, insists on helping me with my fieldwork in Mo Baan. She tells me, over our first portion of noodles, that she has been disowned by her family. 'They sent me to a good school, which is why I speak English. My family had big plans for my career. But then I met Kunal, who I married. He is from Bangladesh, Muslim, and an illegal immigrant here in Thailand.' She looks at me. 'He came to my village selling crêpes with bananas from a little cart. He played guitar and we fell in love. Not long after that, I was pregnant with our first child. But my family didn't accept Kunal and they told the police about the illegal immigrant in town. We had to flee and find a village that my family was unfamiliar with. So now we live here in Mo Baan.'

Ying and I agree that she can help me by becoming my interpreter. She needs a job and wants to do something other than being pregnant and watching children. So Ying sits on the scooter or walks in front of me, very pregnant and dripping with sweat, going from house to house at twilight, when people are home from their work in the fields. She hurls rocks at the village's aggressive and barking dogs and she helps me to find and interview the families where a woman – a mother, sister or daughter – left for Denmark or another European country.

Ying and Kunal live in a sweltering tin shed with their little son, beside the main road's rushing buses and rusty trucks. Kunal is a friendly man, who plucks a chicken and roasts it over the fire for my family. But it is not long before he starts to express his dissatisfaction that Ying's working with me. This means that he has to take care of their son. Ying has become a working mother for a period of time and now she speaks about back when she went to school, about Thai politics and about how people are still poor. It is as if each day we work together, more of the way she used to be comes out. To avoid Kunal becoming upset, we take her little boy with us to our interviews on the scooter, or we carry him. Two mothers going to work with a child and a pregnant belly, to collect data about other women who left this side of the globe to provide for their children.

The author doing fieldwork in Isaan, Thailand

Ghosts

Chai borrows a lacquered wooden dining table from a family with more money, so we don't have to sit on the floor and eat, even though I actually like that better. The villagers grow mushrooms with chicken manure and compost, and the flies love it. Swarms of flies land on any food, on the corners of people's eyes and under children's noses. To get away from the flies, my children want to sit inside at the table, where we can fan them away with old rags and shut the windows. When I can, I go outside and eat under the bamboo porch roof with the women.

In the afternoon, we sit on the cool blue tiles by the entrance to our house. We eat grilled corn that Bun picked in their field. It is getting dark. There is a comfort at twilight, when the day's work is done and only darkness and sleep await. I ask about their neighbours.

Across the red dirt road from Chai and Bun's house stands a two-storey purple house with two golden lions in front, guarding a tall golden gate. It opens by remote control. A woman lives in the house, while her daughter is married to an older man in England and sends money home to her mother. Several times I have seen the mother ride around on her pink bike with a large pink straw hat on her head. She stands there watering her flower beds, which look like they belong in Danish suburbia. The colours are pleasing and there are no weeds. She sweeps the paved courtyard and takes care of a little shrine with fresh flowers and incense. Next door stands a traditional Isaan wooden house with a courtyard and chickens, barking dogs, junk, gnawed cobs of dried-up corn and old tyres.

'Only ghosts live there,' says Chai, when I ask him about another building – a worn-down, yellow, neighbours' house with dirty windows and blue, sun-bleached curtains pulled shut. 'It has been empty for ten years and no one dares to move in and live with the ghosts. The owner moved to another village for work and the sister went abroad, but didn't send any money back home. Since then, the house has been occupied by the grandmother's ghost,' Chai continues, as if it were common knowledge. 'Sometimes you can see her peeking out from behind the curtains. There are several ghosts in the village,' he goes on, telling me about two girls, around twelve or thirteen years old, who drowned in a deep watering hole in the village many years ago. The three girls went down to the water together. One girl couldn't swim and the other one tried to save her. They both drowned. And since then, no one has swum in that watering hole, because the ghosts of the girls could grab their legs and pull them under. In another place there is a tree where a man hung himself. No one goes near that tree anymore.

I recognise this fear of ghosts from my fieldwork in Thy. After a Thai woman died in a car accident on the way home from work, on the highway between Hanstholm and Hurup, none of the women drive that road any more. There are stories about ghosts spread all throughout my notebooks.

'We heard about ghosts from when we were kids,' Sommai told me. 'When someone died in the village, even if of old age, we didn't go outside at all. We didn't have bathrooms in the houses and always peed outside, except for those nights when someone died. Then we brought a pail inside for peeing. But when we travel abroad, we change. At first I was terrified,' she said, 'when we drove past Thisted Cemetery. But I'm not any more. Or only sometimes . . . Remember the woman who was stabbed to death by a client in front of her massage parlour? I drove to the hospital in Skejby to visit her, but I wasn't allowed in because she was so disfigured. But on the way home in the car, I felt that she was sitting right behind me. The week before, she and I had gone out to collect oysters in the Limfjord. We were so close and I had just talked with her recently. When I made it to my driveway, I jumped out and peed my pants I was so scared. I didn't make it inside to the toilet.'

'People are afraid of ghosts,' says Chai, nodding towards the yellow house. 'They are afraid that the dead are not happy in the land of the dead and that they come back to bring the living with them.'

Bun Khun

A few days later, I visit the mother of one of the girls who drowned in the watering hole and who is now – according to the locals – a ghost. I have seen the mother tramping around in her apron with a broom, as she sweeps and cleans for families in the village who own land or whose wives and daughters have travelled overseas for work. She has one daughter left now – Noo, who is fifteen. I walk to their home, away from the main street to the outer edge of the village, where the dirt roads and damp bogs make it cheap to live. Noo sets out water bottles and small bags of crisps for me. She wants to travel so she doesn't have to work in the fields or marry a Thai man with no money. After her sister died, she is her mother's only hope. Noo asks if I can take her back with us to Denmark. She doesn't care which country it is, she just wants to get away.

'My mother wants a house,' says Noo, 'but I'm not sure if I'm pretty enough for a white man.' She touches my arm and says she thinks her skin is too dark. 'My parents are old. My mother is fifty-three. So it should happen soon.'

I think about my male friends back in Nørrebro who are studying at the university, who are taking adult education classes, who want to write books and play music. Would one of them marry Noo when she's old enough to get a visa? I tell her, 'I'm sorry, but I do not know any available men.'

I invite Noo and five or six other girls back to Ying's place. A few days later, after speaking with their parents, the girls and I are sitting on plastic mats in a circle on the tile floor. One of the young girls is what Thais call a 'kathoey' or 'ladyboy', born a boy. She has a white powdered face, pink lipstick, a necklace, a white hairband and is wearing a girl's school uniform. She is well-spoken and cheerful, the child of the village leader. She brings a sense of ease to the otherwise uncertain mood. What was it I wanted to talk to them about?

In my notebook from the meeting, I find their answers, written down concisely from listening to them. I also have a longer tape recording. But in the notebook, their answers are a kind of a wish list for their lives.

Sine: Where would you like to live in the future?

Answers: Bangkok or a foreign country.

Sine: What work would you do or go to school for?

Answers: Doctor, teacher, designer, nurse, stewardess with Thai Airways. (No one wants to work on the farms.)

Sine: What means the most to you in your life?

Answers: Family. (They all said they would send money home to their families.)

These are dreams, hopes and wishes, but with built-in expectations. They dream about travelling and working, and they hope that their fantasies come true. But their family means the most to them and they will send them the money they earn. They want to leave behind the hard work in the fields, where they have seen their parents' skin grow dark and leathery under the merciless sun. They want to leave behind the rough hands that seem out of place with the nail polish they currently wear. They would rather take the bus to Bangkok and find work at a factory, where some people they know already work on assembly lines. The education they want to have is expensive. The people from the village who study at the university have parents who own a lot of land, or they have a sister or mother abroad who sends money back home.

The young ladyboy wants to go to Bangkok and become a doctor. She doesn't want to go to Europe. I ask why not, since all the others want to. She explains that she wants to come back and work in the village, as soon as she finishes her education. She looks serious and adds, 'because of bun khun.'

The others nod and look at her approvingly. Bun khun is a powerful bond that connects the parents in Mo Baan with their children. It is based on the Buddhist concepts of duty and indebtedness. Their parents gave them life and the children don't just owe them lifelong gratitude and respect, but also their active assistance – increasingly as they get older. Sons can fulfil their bun khun duty by becoming monks for a short period, but daughters are not able to do that. Daughters, especially the youngest, can fulfil their bun khun by respectful obedience of their parents' authority and through their contributions to the family. According to most of the girls, the women of Mo Baan can do this best by travelling abroad and working.

Even though bun khun is changing in modern Thailand, it remains important to the women in Thy and Isaan. They send money home to their families and express a strong sense of connection with them. While I was in Mo Baan, and also among the Thai women in Thy, I only heard about two women who stopped sending money home. One was because her father used the money for drinking and the other was because her Danish husband wanted her to stop. But later she started to send money home covertly.

In the same notebook as the list of answers from the young women, I find a forgotten wish list for my own life from that time. I have always made plans and written lists. When I need to organise my thoughts, I write them down systematically in a list. Things I have to do and goals I want to reach.

This one had the heading: *Sine's Dreams.*

- Live in New York
- Get a PhD
- Work for a charity in another country
- Live eco-friendly and cheaply
- Have friends
- Live near a city
- Organic food
- Time for children
- Laugh
- Love

These two lists – the one with the answers from the young women and my own – are nearly side by side in my notebook. The list from the young women is about dreams and duty to family, while my list is primarily about myself and my little family. The young women are thinking about their lifelong responsibilities as daughters. There is nothing about being a daughter on my list. I don't have to send money back home to my parents and I'm not economically responsible for their old age. My parents have pensions from a long life of steady work. They live in a wealthy society with nursing homes and free hospitals. In Thailand, the women's parents are day labourers and a pension is about 600 baht[10] per month, enough for food for four or five days. Serious illnesses like cancer can't be treated in the rural hospitals and treatment has to be paid for, if possible, at private hospitals.

Ten years later, I look at these lists while I am in New York, with my PhD, and I know that none of these young women have received the education they dreamed of. They went to Bangkok to work in a factory or to Pattaya to work in tourism; some of them in the sex industry. Two of them are married in Europe. I am in my second marriage.

With the lists, I find a note from Ying, written two days after our focus group meeting. 'I am going to the hospital today. I will be gone for three days. Can you come over?' On the back, she drew four hearts and a hot sun in orange.

The note is from when Ying went to the hospital for three days to give birth to the child she was pregnant with when we drove around Mo Baan. I remember visiting her at the little local hospital after her baby was born. He was a little boy wearing yellow mittens and a yellow cap. By the bed rail lay a yellow towel and a gold-leaf-ornamented letter from the Thai Prime Minister, Thaksin Shinawatra. It read, 'Thank you for giving Thailand one more citizen. Welcome.'

At the time, Thaksin, also called the Berlusconi of Asia, was trying to gain support among the poor populations in north-east Thailand by delivering birth letters and by building motorways. New mothers received thanks for bringing children into the country,

[10] 14 GBP

despite the fact that thousands of women had to travel abroad or sell sex in order to support them.

Ying and Kunal went on to have four children. Then, people in the village started to hear cries and tumult from their house. Kunal was beating Ying. One day, they left the village to sell crêpes to the tourists in Pattaya. I never saw Ying again. I still look for her whenever I pass a crêpe cart in Pattaya.

Five Kilos of Rice

One early morning in Mo Baan, an older woman with a stern gaze, work boots and a wide straw hat is standing in front of our house. She is Pen, the wealthy village landowner. Sommai told me about her several times before I left for Mo Baan. Now she is standing here because she wants to show me something. We walk over to her big house by the intersection.

In front of her house, there are two trucks full of cassava roots, ready to be driven to the Chinese-owned factory down the highway, where they will be processed into starch to be used in instant ramen. We drive in her air-conditioned pickup truck down muddy red roads out to her fields. I am unsure what she wants. She tells me in detail about what she is growing in the fields, the prices of the crops and what she pays her workers. The day labourers, most of whom I know from the village, receive 60 baht[11] to work from eight in the morning, through the heat of the day, until five in the evening. They can also earn extra based on how many kilos they harvest. It is seasonal work and the day labourers have trouble finding work outside of the planting and harvesting seasons. So they have to pick a lot, and the money has to last until the next season.

When we drive back to the village, Pen asks me if I could help her daughter find a husband. She is actually

[11] 1 GBP

getting a business degree in Bangkok, but there aren't many jobs for a young woman in the countryside when she's done. And even though the family has money, they don't have any real contacts in Europe, which is why she is asking me, she says. I tell her that I don't know anyone looking for a Thai wife.

When Sommai talks about Pen back in Thy, she uses a particular tone of voice. It comes from the time before Sommai left for Pattaya. Pen lived diagonally across from Sommai, but Sommai's house was much smaller and was shared by more people. One day, Sommai's large family had so little money and so little food that Sommai crossed the street to see if she could borrow five kilos of rice. Pen said no.

'I was so ashamed,' said Sommai. 'I had to bicycle far to the next village, in the heat, to borrow rice for my children.'

The shame she felt when Pen turned her down is what finally got Sommai to write the note to her father.

Where the Earth is Black With Rain

On my drive with Pen, I realise that the families of the migrant women from Mo Baan are the only ones, apart from the few landowners like Pen, who can afford a newly built house. Mo Baan is not special; it is a typical Isaan village. Founded in 1952 by a family of about fifty people who moved from a neighbouring village, it has grown to a population of about 550. Until 2003, the village shared a communal water pump at the school, but when Sommai left for Europe, the village began to change, due to the money that she and other women who followed her sent back home. Seventeen women have left Mo Baan for Europe. The village leader, Sanan, shows me a map of the houses in Mo Baan and points out those that were paid for by migrant women. Down the road in another village similar in size to Mo Baan, fifteen women have left. And in the next village, twenty women.

Most villages in Isaan have what the residents call 'farang' houses – houses financed by marrying a foreigner or by sex work. The new houses are not built like the traditional dwellings in the village. They have glass-paned windows, concrete, acrylic paint and caulked, sealed joints. The bathrooms and kitchen are brought inside the house – along with their heavy smell of moisture. The air is stagnant, as air-conditioning is expensive to install, as is electricity. But some of the women who now live in Denmark have had air-conditioning installed in the rooms they sleep in when they are home visiting the village.

In contrast to the farang houses, traditional houses are wood, without glass panes in the windows, but with shutters instead, so the night's cooler breezes can waft through the house. They are built on stilts, so there is space and shade for animals underneath. During the hottest periods, the older villagers sleep outside on old wooden beds beneath mosquito netting. These elders, parents of the women who leave, are often those for whom the new houses are built.

The Thai author Kampoon Boontawee writes in one of his most famous books, *A Child of the Northeast*, about life in Isaan in the 1930s.[viii] I read it in Mo Baan in the evenings before I go to sleep, when the village is quiet, while the fan blows across my face and over the mattress on the floor. At one point, he writes about drought-stricken ghost towns, which people have left, while the boy, Koon (the author), and his family are left behind. The boy asks his mother, 'Where are the uncles going?' His mother answers, 'To the place where the earth is black with rain, and fish strike the water like the tails of crocodiles.'

Tales from Isaan of the 1930s, 1940s and 1950s reveal migration as a courageous decision with serious causes. People rarely travelled alone back then, but as a family. The woman's role was to pack the belongings and prepare food for the trip, and they sat in the ox-cart while the men walked alongside.

In the 1960s, 1970s and 1980s, people in the villages started travelling alone to seek work. Today, many of the female migrants from Mo Baan are daughters of male migrants who borrowed money for a ticket to Bangkok, or sometimes to Singapore, Taiwan or Saudi

Arabia. But today, the male migrants from Isaan, who typically drive taxis in Bangkok, build skyscrapers in Malaysia or tend animals in New Zealand, earn less than the women in Europe. The women, in contrast to the men, can often live in a house in a foreign country while building a house in their home village or sending money to their families.

'The women here are like heroes,' says the village leader. 'If the village or the temple is in need of something, I ask the families with a woman in Europe first. Because these women have been the most fortunate compared to the other migrants,' he says.

The hope that migrants who leave the village will send something back to those left behind is nothing new. In Boontawee's book, the boy Koon says, 'One day, when yet another family left the village, I asked a woman, "If there is a lot of fish there, remember us. Could you send back a big one, if someone comes back to visit?"'

'Remember us.' That phrase touches me when I read it one evening. Back then, they dreamed that the migrants would return with food, whereas today Thai women send home money. They remember the people they left behind.

A traditional house in Isaan

A 'farang' house in Isaan built using money sent home by women living abroad

Lom

Pattaya, 2007

I want to meet Lom. She has often been mentioned in my conversations about women who have left the village and her absence is somehow palpable. Lom left the village to work in Pattaya when she was sixteen. When I return to Thailand in 2007, I call her. We decide to meet a few days later and I take the bus from the village to Pattaya. Lom has suggested a cafe on the main street.

Lom is wearing a short, white dress with large grey and pink polka dots. Her hair is black, in a pageboy cut and she is wearing false eyelashes. She orders a cola while I have coffee. When I tell her that I came to Pattaya just to talk to her, she says, 'That makes me feel special. Normally, no one does anything just for me.' I try to explain that I want to ask her about her life, because I am researching the lives of women in Pattaya and the lives of women who want to go abroad. So, in a way, I am also there for my own sake. 'The most important thing is that you have been in my village. So you can ask me anything you want.'

Lom says that she is a 'freelancer', not attached to a specific bar. Every night she looks for clients among young tourists at the big dance clubs. She often doesn't come home until nearly morning. About every five minutes during our conversation, she pulls out a little make-up kit with a mirror from her handbag and checks her eye make-up, then her hair and sometimes she puts on a new layer of lip gloss and mascara. It gives me a feeling of intimacy and openness, that she checks herself right in front of me while I'm watching. Since then, I have seen Lom do this in all kinds of situations – looking in her mirror or checking messages from her clients on her phone. She is always working.

When we leave the cafe after about two hours of talking, she takes my hand, something she will do for many years to come, and leads me confidently through Pattaya's hot air and intense traffic to her room on the outskirts of the city. Here is where many of the young women from Isaan live. Lom stops at a long building that resembles a barracks, with a metal roof and lots of small rooms. The entrances are off a long, covered porch. She recently moved here with Lek, a woman from a neighbouring village. The two women share a small room, with a double bed that fills most of it. The mattress is covered with thick plastic, so it can be cleaned easily with a rag. Synthetic pillows in blue and green terry cloth with dingy corners are in a pile on the bed. There is also an adjacent toilet in the back, with a hose and a cement tub to wash in.

On the wall, drawings with red handwriting on them are hung up with tape and clothes hang on plastic hangers from a rope running across the room. Lek is standing in front of a mirror, trying on a pair of new tight jeans. We have never met before. I ask if she bought the jeans at the market today. 'Yes, with a client. He gets turned on if I pee in my pants,' she says, making a face. 'I do it if he buys me a new pair of trousers each time, so now I have a new pair of jeans,' she says triumphantly.

Lom's plan today is to set long extensions in her short hair. Maybe she just thought of it when she met

Lom and her friend in Pattaya

me. I learn that Lom is a quick-thinking businesswoman in her own way. She asks if I will come with her and if I will pay for it. It's a deal. This will give me a chance to see this side of her work in Pattaya. We walk along narrow alleys to a little salon, where young women are sitting in chairs getting long, black hair extensions. I sit down on a pink sofa and wait while they attach the extensions to Lom's scalp. I can see from the hairdresser's face that she can't figure out what I'm doing there with Lom. In Pattaya, you see all kinds of couples – women with men, men with men, men with ladyboys. An anthropologist with a sex worker is not a common one. But women buy sex too, mostly from men, and the hairdresser seems to place Lom and me in that category. I am a female farang client, a foreigner, and Lom is a sex worker.

There is an unexpected bang, almost a crash, from the window. Outside, there is a group of boys, ten- to twelve-year-olds in flip-flops, shorts and T-shirts, banging hard on the large window. 'There they are again,' shouts one of the hairdressers angrily. Two hairdressers run outside. One has a broom and she yells at the boys while holding it threateningly. They run off, but two minutes later they are back in front of the salon. Lom says they are children who live in Pattaya with their mothers, but who have white, European fathers. They are children of clients. I had noticed that the boys had lighter skin.

On the way back from the salon, we turn down Walking Street, where women stroll the beachfront pavement offering sex. Suddenly, traffic is stopped by a demonstration of about a hundred children who are wandering towards the street. On the edges of the protest are grown women, helping the children with their signs and making sure they keep together. Lom says that this is a demonstration for children like those we saw in front of the salon. 'They have foreign fathers,' she says. 'They are the children of women and their clients.' Some of them are wearing costumes that look like condoms. Others are holding coffins with the word 'Mum' written on them. Others are carrying signs that say, 'Access to better health care for all', 'Our mothers are also people', 'Stop AIDS', 'Stop stigma' and 'Don't hate the sick, hate the sickness'. It is 1 December, World AIDS Day. These are the children of sex workers, marching against AIDS on behalf of their sick and dead mothers. I get a lump in my throat when they pass by towards the go-go bars.

Lom takes my hand and we walk back to her apartment. Lek and Lom eat, wash and put on their make-up. Lom styles her new hair, pulls on short denim shorts, stilettos and a tight blouse and they walk together down the road to work on Walking Street.

Transactional Relationships

I paid for Lom's hair extensions. Since then, I have paid for false eyelashes, manicures, parts of airline tickets, school uniforms, doctor visits, money for a new visa, debts to neighbours and much more. I have helped out often. Not just Lom, but the other women I have worked with too. They need to earn money for food for their children, for clothes and a place to live – and so they can send money home to their families. That is the purpose of their sex work and they rarely take time off.

Most sex workers sleep until late afternoon, when it's time to eat and get ready for the evening. They hardly have any time in between. They are constantly looking for clients, and sometimes my presence has meant that they have had to postpone a client or go to work later to have time to talk with me. I compensate them for their lost wages.

Part of our relationship is transactional. They answer my questions, take me with them into settings where I otherwise would not have access, and I compensate them for their time. Time, knowledge and access is valuable. I am building my research, my career, upon knowledge that I have gained by working with these women. To me it would be absurd if I didn't also contribute in the other direction. I don't have the resources to fundamentally change their lives, but I can help them when they are in need, when it counts.

In order to continue my research into migration

and global sex, I have to return to the women, follow their paths over time. The doors that they hold open for me to an otherwise closed world must not shut. I don't believe the myth that money changing hands between us impacts the stories being told. That is an elitist myth, because it has most often been the person with the economic surplus who has defined the idea that money colours knowledge and potentially falsifies answers. This is an abstract equation that does not agree with the reality of my daily work as an anthropologist. My research is open and thorough. It touches all my relationships, which often become deeper and deeper, and, as they have with the women in this book, sometimes turn into lifelong friendships. Of course, money plays a role.

Those Who Are Left Behind

Mo Baan, 2007

When I return to the village, I visit Lom's mother, Samarn. Lom's family lives across from the house that Sommai had built in the village. Samarn has bought two small bags of crisps and a sweet yogurt drink from the little grocery for my visit. We sit down on a blue sofa with a plastic cover. On the coffee table is a grey telephone with grimy buttons and next to it a wrinkled piece of paper with six or seven phone numbers for her daughter who lives in England. There are doodles and food stains on the paper. It appears to be an important document, one that is always left out. The telephone sits there as if it were a member of the family.

I tell Samarn that I met Lom in Pattaya and that she is doing well. 'OK,' says Samarn, without changing her expression. 'Lom is my middle daughter. She is always difficult. She does what she wants, but she never sends money home.' As she offers me the yogurt drink, there is a charged mood in the air. I know that Lom has siblings and when I ask about them, Samarn continues, 'You might know that my eldest daughter is married in England with a man she met in Pattaya. Since then, she found a husband for Lom in England. Lom had been working in Pattaya since the free years of schooling ended. We couldn't afford to send her to school, so we borrowed money for her ticket and sent her to England, because she wanted to go there too. And it would be better for us if she got married there.

But Lom left England and came back to the village after a few months.'

Lom told me that she returned to Thailand because it was grey and lonely in England. When her husband went to work, she stayed in bed and cried. She was used to the bustle of Pattaya, to being out every night and sharing her room with several young women like her. They slept in the same bed, bought street food and ate together. But in England, her sister lived far away and, without a work permit, Lom couldn't do anything except stay at home.

Lom didn't think her husband was very nice and he wasn't really interested in her, just in sex. So she went into debt for a ticket to leave England. Her sister wouldn't pay for it and her family thought that Lom had wasted the chance of her life; that she was spoiled and expected more from a husband and from England than was realistic.

Samarn asks me, 'Why couldn't she just have adapted and accepted it? Now she's back where she started, in Pattaya.'

Samarn shows me around her house. It is a new house paid for by her daughter in England, with blue tiles on the floor, three bedrooms, a kitchen and a bathroom. One room in the house has air-conditioning. It's locked. 'Lom can't use this room, since she doesn't send money home,' says Samarn, as if it was obvious, since electricity for air-conditioning is too expensive. I write in my notebook: 'Lom is the problem child. Air-conditioning is for the big sister when she visits from England. Lom's little sister is studying to be a tour guide in the nearest state capital. Her big sister in England is paying for it.'

We sit back down on the blue sofa. I say that Sommai

told me how the two of them, she and Samarn, went to Pattaya together many years ago and how Sommai, after she wrote the note to her father and put her kids on the bus back to her parents, met Samarn at the bus station. 'Yes, Sommai and I were childhood friends,' she says. 'At that point, I didn't have children and I had a Thai boyfriend. He was crazy about me, but I wanted more than the life he could offer me here in Mo Baan. He wasn't wealthy. Pattaya sounded tempting and an easy way to make money. Sommai and I took the bus together and lived in a room over the bar. But I didn't have many clients. I wasn't very pretty and I didn't like being there. After a few weeks, my boyfriend came to Pattaya to get me and I returned with him to Mo Baan. He is Lom's father and the father of my children. I stayed here.'

I Would Rather Sell Sex Than Work For the UN

Bangkok, 2007

The next week, I travel to Bangkok to work on a UN project that is researching what happens to women who return to Thailand and the Philippines after trafficking. Every day, at an organisation in central Bangkok, we hold meetings about impoverished women in a neighbourhood where expats from the UN and international firms eat lunch at expensive French restaurants and drink white wine. Even though I eat Isaan food at a cheaper local restaurant, I feel so far away from Mo Baan.

I call Lom from my hotel and ask if she wants to come to Bangkok and stay with me at the hotel for a few days. The room has two beds and comes with breakfast and a swimming pool. Would she like a little break? She arrives on the bus that evening in her work clothes. Tight shorts, black eye make-up and a short top with a pink print. We check her into the hotel, where the receptionist looks a bit confused. We are used to that by now.

Up in the room, Lom tells me she's pregnant and that she doesn't have the money for an abortion. That was partly why she said yes to coming to Bangkok so fast. Without knowing, I called her at a critical moment. We have to think quickly. At that time – and until 2021 – abortions were illegal in Thailand, except under special circumstances such as rape or when serious issues are detected in the foetus. Women like Lom could face up to three years in prison and a fine equivalent to an inconceivable £1,500, but Lom knows a place in Bangkok where she can have it done. So the next day we go to an illegal abortion clinic.

The clinic is located behind a high wall with lush trees in the yard. Girls and women are sitting in a row on plastic chairs while they wait to be called. Lom is afraid of getting caught. Then it's Lom's turn. She comes out half an hour later, walking slowly and with difficulty. We take a taxi back to the hotel. She lies down with a sanitary pad between her legs and a pillow on her belly, while I go out and get some food for us. Later, I ask her if I should ask one of the organisations I am working with to see if they can help her. She can't work right after the abortion and she will have nowhere to live upon her return to Pattaya as she can't afford her room with Lek. I can give her a bit of money, but I can't support her long-term or find her a place to live. Maybe she could go to one of the organisations' crisis centres. Lom agrees.

I schedule a time with a Thai social worker, who will come and see Lom at our room the next day. Lom is nervous. She asks me, 'What should I do to get the woman to help me?' She suggests that she not put on her make-up. Then, when the woman comes to see her, she will look more sick than she really feels. Lom always wears make-up, even back in her village, but she is afraid that if she does so here, the woman from the crisis centre won't think her problems are bad enough to deserve help. I say that a woman like her, who sells sex, just had an abortion, has no place to live and can't work, ought to be able to get assistance without looking sick.

While I'm off working the next day, the woman comes to our hotel-room door and offers Lom a spot at their crisis centre in Bangkok. They provide food and a bed – but not work or money. Lom turns it down; she has to earn money.

When I return to the room in the evening, Lom is lying on the bed with her two phones, flirting with her clients. She is trying to get them to send her money from wherever they are in the world. They have returned home from their vacations in Pattaya and are back in their daily routines, while she tries to get them to hold on to their memories. In her sweetest voice, she says to them, 'Remember the time we had.'

She has bought street food in little plastic bags. I remove my work shirt and my sweaty shoes and lie down on the bed. I'm exhausted after an hour in Bangkok's busy streets and a day of meetings about human trafficking. My brain is both buzzing and shutting down. I ask her if it's stressful to have two telephones and so many clients to keep track of. While she continues to navigate between clients, she says, 'No, it's my job. I don't understand how you manage your job. It must be stressful to have to show up at a certain time and to have so many meetings. And to have to write so much and speak in front of other people. And it doesn't seem fun at all. And you're not in charge.' She says, 'I wouldn't want your job at the UN.'

Ten days after her abortion, Lom takes the bus back to Pattaya.

Ghost Hotel Rooms

Pattaya, 2007

Lom moves in with her girlfriend Lek again, to a residential complex on the edge of Pattaya. It is modern, peach-coloured and expensive. They share a double bed, a closet, a mirror, a little bathroom and the rent.

I am sitting on the floor with Lom and Lek, eating with a spoon and fork out of flower-patterned bowls. They bought street food for us on the corner and we are drinking cola from large plastic cups.

I ask how work is going lately. 'The clients know too much now,' says Lom. 'Many of them have been in Pattaya lots of times before, or they have friends who have been here. You can't tell them anything. They ask questions, haggle on the price. If I can say no to them, I do. Experienced clients are difficult. I have been working here a long time and I'm good at sensing what a client wants. The best are the ones who are grateful that you're going with them; the ones who are a bit nervous and new. I also like black Americans, or black people in general. They are handsome. The worst ones are the ones who smell, or are drunk.'

The food has been eaten and Lek is lying on the bed, looking at her phone. Lom continues, 'And I don't go with them if I'm not sure there is only one client,' she says. 'You know, when you come up to the room and there are two guys sitting there waiting. It's hard to know. That has happened to me several times. But I turn right around in the door, because I don't know what they could be up to. They get all kinds of ideas when they're together.'

'If there are several clients to choose from, I choose by the hotel,' says Lek, from the bed. 'If the client is staying at a nice hotel, then he has more money and then maybe I get more nights out of it . . . And I don't want to go somewhere where the receptionist and the guard glare at us. They know what we're doing there.'

'And then there are some hotels with ghosts,' says Lom. 'The clients don't know it, but if another girl or a farang died in a room at a hotel, I try not to go there.'

'How do they die?' I ask.

'Some girls who went to a room with several clients were found dead,' says Lom. 'Some took drugs with the client; some girls jumped off the balcony and committed suicide. Some of the old farangs die during sex. They take Viagra and can't handle it.'

There is a tone of care and respect in Lom's voice. She doesn't want to work in a room as if it were 'business as usual' if a woman like herself has suffered and died there.

These are not just stories. Local newspapers like *Pattaya Mail* regularly print articles about women and men who have died in the city. A receptionist told me once that no one would book the hotel rooms where someone had died. The hotel always hides it and hopes that it will be forgotten. I think about that conversation sometimes when I shut the door behind me in a new hotel room in Pattaya.

Lom and Lek start preparing for their night of work. It takes a couple of hours. First a bath, then ironing their outfits with the tiled floor as an ironing board. They wear dresses or short shorts and a top. They wear false eyelashes, which last for two to three weeks if they are careful with them and don't let the water from the shower get in their eyes. These are an expensive part of the work uniform. It takes time to apply mascara carefully to the long lashes without clumping. Their hair must be smoothed out. Sometimes they affix a little artificial diamond to a tooth. They apply body lotion, touch up their fingernail and toenail polish. They often try on three or four outfits and discuss them with each other.

They find most of their clients among the young tourists at Lucifer, a gigantic, cave-like nightclub with several floors in the middle of Walking Street. Lucifer's advertisements have pictures of Thai, Latin American and Russian women in black bikinis with red, devilish tridents. 'Dance at the ultimate Pattaya club,' they read. 'The doors open at ten, but there is no reason to get there before one in the morning,' explains Lom. 'The men have to be tipsy, horny and already starting to look for the woman they want to take back to their room for the night.'

I meet Lek again several years later, when she is six months pregnant, her round belly projecting out from her tall, thin body. She is taking amphetamines now and wants to have an abortion. She asks if she can borrow money for it. In my notebook, I write that I am not sure if I should lend her the money. The feotus, the baby, is big now. I feel like an accomplice, but at the same time, it is her choice. I ask if I could take care of her baby for a while if she decides to have it. But Lek is afraid that she'll miss her baby if someone else is taking care of it. She doesn't dare tell her parents she is pregnant by one of her clients. She knows that her family will be even harder pressed if she leaves her baby with her mother, her father and the family she is already trying to support.

Lek wants to have an abortion no matter what, even if it is at an illegal, cheap clinic, where her life could be in danger. This is a very difficult situation, one that I will think about many times over the years. But I see no other way to help than to give her some of the money, so she can have it done at a safer clinic. Lek goes there alone. She didn't want me to come and I sense that Lom didn't want to go with her. I try to find out where she went afterwards, but I don't find out before she is back in Pattaya.

Several years later, Lom tells me that Lek is in the infamous women's section of Pattaya's remand prison for selling amphetamines.

Rest and Recreation

One evening, Lom takes me to Lucifer. While she is on the dance floor or walking watchfully among the tables, smiling, flirting and professionally catching every interested glance, I am standing at the bar with a beer. The club is filled with American soldiers deployed to Afghanistan, who right now are on 'rest and recreation' in Pattaya. Several times, I have seen flocks of soldiers arrive at Walking Street, with its promenade bathed in red lights, while women call to them from inside the bars. It's like a scene from a Hollywood Vietnam film, when the soldiers walk down the middle of the street, while the women call out, 'Hello, sexy man . . .'

At one of the oldest bars in Pattaya, one of the walls is plastered with framed, faded wedding photos of American soldiers in uniform and Thai women in white, puffy wedding dresses, often in front of vintage American cars. Sex, war and capitalism have helped to form Pattaya but some people also found love here many years ago. There are also thank-you notes from American generals hanging up. They are thanking the bar's owner for taking care of the American soldiers. There are letters from Vietnam, Iraq and Afghanistan.

These soldiers are different from the older white men in shorts, with big bellies and sleeveless undershirts, who go to Pattaya for a three-week vacation and sit across from a Thai woman, eating fried eggs and white toast in the hotel's restaurant, the morning after. The soldiers are young and well-trained, and more racially diverse than the tourists. I remember Lom telling me that her favourite clients are black American soldiers. They seem like groups of friends visiting the city and the young Thai women prefer them as clients.

One of the soldiers comes over to me at the bar. We drink a beer. I dance with him and he says that he likes thin women like me. He keeps talking about what kind of women he likes. It feels awkward. He tells me he likes Thai women – they like to have fun, they smile and they aren't dismissive like the women in bars at home. It seems like he chooses to ignore the fact that the women at the bar here smile at him because they are working and they want him as a client. It all feels so innocent, as if everyone is pretending to be on vacation – the women too, even though Lom is working hard to get a client for the night. An illusory game, and he is falling for it.

Maybe I seem interesting to him because I don't quite fit in. The women who are working are much younger, more flirtatious and more sexily dressed than I am. Just like when Lom's hairdresser had trouble placing me. I am out of context; a white woman drinking beer and asking him about the war in Afghanistan. He seems both attracted and hesitant, as if he doesn't know if I would be free to him, or if I am checking to see if I can get money out of him. Lom wouldn't speak to him for a second without already having calculated the possibilities. One night? All night? Or a girlfriend-type relationship for the rest of his vacation? To her, he means work. For me, he is a random flirt, and with my constant anthropology lens, he is an insight, data. We dance and drink more beer, but I do not go back to his hotel.

I travel back home from Thailand a few days later. Lom remains in Pattaya and several years pass before I see her again.

Debt

Copenhagen 2007–2008

After my fieldwork, I arrive one cold winter night to a half-finished renovation project at our apartment in Nørrebro. Morten has been home with the boys. Pattaya is still coursing through my body. It gives me a rush to do fieldwork, to sit listening intensely, taking in details, writing; the excitement when I suddenly see a connection. This time, it has affected me more. I am surprised that I talked so much with that soldier. I don't usually do that; I never have before. I see myself as loyal and faithful. But Pattaya is a place without boundaries, a place of forgetting for so many of the men I have spoken with. They go there to forget their often hard work and daily life in Western Europe. And now I feel like I have seen a glimpse of this, as if I have felt the rush of oblivion for a moment. As if the forgetting were contagious.

But in Nørrebro, the oval mirror I just bought for our new apartment has been broken. The new bathroom floor has to be removed again, because the radiant heating isn't working. Our whole family has to go to the toilet in a bucket or go down to the courtyard from the fourth floor. Our very young carpenters have discovered that the roof tiles are loose on this old building and each one has to be reattached before the additions to the roof can be built. Morten is tired after taking care of the children while I have been away, right in the middle of a remodelling project that is dragging on.

Until now, we have lived like a couple of students in a tiny apartment with two children, all of us sleeping in the same room, or with us adults sometimes sleeping in the living room. We are going crazy from living on top of each other. The children keep growing and we really need more space. But we know nothing about building and it is costing a fortune, more than we planned. The bank keeps saying yes to increasing loans, not just to us, but to many people in the years leading up to the financial crisis. We are trying to push through, but it is wearing us down.

We end up with a beautiful, expensive apartment and when the financial crisis starts a few months later, our interest spikes from 4.25% to 8% almost overnight. It is alarming and impossible to repay. Suddenly, it's as if the abstract numbers on the bank papers have turned into real money, but twice as much as we agreed to. International trends and speculators in the financial sector have created a housing bubble that has burst and we are left helpless in the mess. We owe much too much and we earn too little.

Debt eats away at us. Before we go to sleep, it gnaws at our thoughts until there is room for nothing else. It gnaws at our relationship. Debt feels like an illness. Morten and I are growing distant; the cracks are getting too big. We decide to get divorced, and it is terrible.

Many months before, I had sent PhD applications to universities in England and New York, with a proposal about the trafficking of Nigerian women, with fieldwork in Nigeria and Copenhagen. One afternoon, I get a call from a professor in New York. 'Am I speaking with Mrs Plambech?'

'Yes,' I say, hesitantly.

‘I am calling to congratulate you. You have been accepted.’ The voice talks and talks. ‘We are looking forward to seeing you this fall in New York.’

This is my dream come true. PhD, New York, adventure, the big, wide world. And at the same time, it feels as if the world is disappearing under my feet. I am in the middle of a divorce. I have two children and a huge debt. ‘Thank you, thank you for calling,’ I stammer, then blurt out, ‘I accept. Do you know how to get child care in New York?’

‘No, I don’t,’ says the voice. ‘I’m not the right person to ask about that.’

Dustpan Manoeuvre

Copenhagen, 2009

The female police woman asks, 'Is she fat, or isn't she?' into the radio, to the station coordinating the search. A male voice repeats in a scratchy tone, 'The person in question is heavy-set.'

I am doing fieldwork for my PhD in the red-light district, sitting in the backseat of a police car racing down Istedgade, before taking a left at the main train station, around the block and back again. The two female officers on the seats in front of me are looking for a woman they call Sonia, who is wearing tight white leggings with silver rivets down the sides. They say that Sonia is from Nigeria and she is wanted for human trafficking. She is suspected of being a madam and for recruiting women from Nigeria to cross the Sahara Desert, the Mediterranean Sea to Sicily, and then across the borders of Europe, to end up at Istedgade, where they sell sex.

The police catch a glimpse of a pair of white-clad, heavy-set legs behind a van, silver rivets sparkling with reflections from the streetlights. They hit the brakes hard and jump out of the car. 'Come with us,' they say, and I run after them.

A group of black women is running away, through gates, across streets, out towards the lakes where it is dark and there are bushes to hide in. Soon afterwards, a tall, muscular officer appears from around the corner with Sonia in handcuffs. They caught fourteen women in what the police call a 'dustpan manoeuvre'. 'We need another van,' says the male officer over the radio. 'We have more to bring in.' They are all put in handcuffs and searched. They are being detained for selling sex without a work visa.

One woman says to the officer who is searching her, 'My money and passport are in my stockings. Please, can I take out my money?'

Before the dustpan manoeuvre, a plain-clothes officer collected information about the working women. With a hidden camera in his shirt pocket, he walked along Istedgade and collected offers from the unsuspecting women. The police show me the videos. A black woman in tight leggings is flirting with the officer, not knowing that she is looking into a camera. 'Do you want to join me for some fun?' she asks.

'Some fun?' asks the officer. I know that he wants the woman to offer him sex and to say an amount, to prove that she is working illegally – that is, selling sex without a work permit. 'Do you mean sex?' he asks.

'Yes, sex for five hundred,' she answers. And that was the proof he needed. This woman, and the others he got offers from, were working illegally. So the dustpan manoeuvre could be set in motion.

I am standing in front of Danske Bank on the corner of Vesterbrogade, watching the police officers and the women. This is the third time I have gone out with the police at night, but the first time I am witness to a raid. The women are now standing in a row, their cuffed hands on the roof of the police car and their backs on display to the gawking passers-by in the middle of the night in Vesterbro. A taxi driver slams on the brakes, because he can't squeeze past with his passenger. He lifts his hands from the steering wheel,

Nigerian women at work in Copenhagen's red-light district

A woman handcuffed at the police station after the raid

visibly irritated over the women in the road delaying his work.

The police car drives through the metal gate at Station 1, which opens several times over the next hour as the vehicles arrive with more detained women. Here in the early hours, the people being detained are male drug dealers who have been fighting, and then these women – the sex workers.

The women stand in a white hall in the basement of Station 1, in a long row with their handcuffs on, waiting for a hearing. The women who won't say their names, and who have no identification, hold up a white sheet of paper with a question mark for the police photo. They follow an officer into the fingerprinting room, where they do it the old way, with black ink.

A Nigerian woman asks in English, 'Do you only have this old kind? In my country, we have a more modern one.' She laughs. The officer seems a bit perplexed. Time passes. He struggles with the old machine. He can't get the imprint to be precise. The woman asks, 'Can I get a drink of water?'

'Yes, there is water over there.' The officer points to a small sink with a stack of plastic cups.

'Is it safe to drink?' she asks.

The officer looks at her in disbelief. 'Is it safe to drink the water here? Yes, you can drink the water in Denmark.'

'OK, I will. But if I die, it's your fault,' she says, pointing at him.

I am allowed to be present during the questioning. The leader of the dustpan manoeuvre comes in and explains to the interrogating officer that I am allowed to remain and that I 'can know everything'. The first woman is brought in. I sit in the back and observe.

'Where are you from?' asks the female officer.

'Nigeria,' says the woman.

'Where in Nigeria?'

'Benin City.'

'Who ordered and paid for your tickets?'

'I did.'

'Was Spain the first European country you arrived in?'

'Yes, I was there.'

'How did you get here? Did someone arrange your trip, or did you do it alone?'

The Nigerian woman shakes her head.

The officer continues, 'We know that there are people earning money from women working the streets.'

The woman shakes her head again. 'No, you're wrong.'

The officer raises her voice and looks directly at the woman. 'For God's sake, there is no sign at the airport that says come to Vesterbro and be a prostitute. So it would be nice if you told me where you live and who helped you get to Denmark.'

'No one helped me. If I work as a prostitute, I do it for a reason. I have a family. I have children to take care of. So I would like to borrow your phone, please, so I can call my children before they get worried. They can't take care of themselves.'

The officer says, 'I know that you are not working as a prostitute because you want to, that it's because you have to.'[ix]

The woman shakes her head again and starts to cry. The officer makes her a cup of tea, hands her a napkin to dry her eyes and continues, 'If anyone is controlling what you do in Denmark, and if anyone is taking your money, we can help you. We can protect you. But you have to tell us the truth.'

The woman keeps crying. 'What truth do you want?' she whispers.

I wish I could vanish and not be here. No one should be sitting in this room.

Two days later, the *Ekstra Bladet* newspaper writes: 'Fourteen women who are characterised as prostitutes were imprisoned by the Copenhagen magistrate after a raid in Vesterbro, which targeted female Nigerian prostitutes. The purpose was to find the people behind the prostitutes, but information about them has been slim.'[x]

The police explain to me that the 'dustpan manoeuvre' cleans up the streets. 'We are trying to separate the "victims" from the "criminals" – the illegal migrants from the women who are being coerced – and to get them to turn in their pimps.' Instead, twelve of the fourteen women were eventually deported from Denmark. Some were sent to Nigeria, others to Italy.

I Am Being Sent Out of This Country

Kastrup Airport, 2009

A few days later, at six o'clock in the morning, I meet with two plain-clothes officers at a police station in Copenhagen. I am going with them to pick up Ann, a Nigerian woman, who has been imprisoned at Vestre Prison. She is going to be deported after a dustpan manoeuvre on Istedgade. I am sitting in the backseat while the two officers briefly explain their work to me. They pick up foreigners almost every morning and drive them to the airport. The two officers seem to know each other well. They chat about family and holiday plans. At the prison, we drive through the first large, locked, dark green gate. It shuts behind us and then I wait with one officer while the other leaves to get Ann.

A short, stocky woman with cropped hair returns with the officer and is seated next to me. 'Good morning,' I say. She returns my greeting and then sits there, looking at her phone, which has a pink cover. We drive in silence to Vesterbrogade, where Ann had been living in a small room and sharing a bed with two other Nigerian women at one of the often-overlooked migrant boarding houses in Copenhagen centre. I have been here before. An older man whom the women call 'The Frog' runs the boarding house. He makes sure they pay their rent and that it is kept somewhat orderly. But he gets angry when the women make Nigerian food, which makes the little kitchen smell of fish. At her room, one of the officers asks Ann to pack her things. She has no suitcase, just small bags and a large plastic bag. She gathers her small shampoo bottles, her clothes, a pair of boots and other belongings and places them in the bags.

We continue driving to the airport without talking. Ann tries to call from her phone, but either there is no reception or the person is not answering. We enter a private parking area for police and border control. One officer carries Ann's black plastic bag and she walks between them to check in at Scandinavian Airlines' efficient business desk in Terminal 3. Two more officers arrive with a young man who is also being deported. He is wearing a seashell necklace and carrying a drum under his arm. One officer is holding a cardboard box with his belongings. They wait in line behind us.

Ann gets through on her phone and talks with someone while she walks to the gate between the two officers. I hear her say that she is on her way to the plane. 'I am being sent out of this country,' she explains. On the way to the gate, she exchanges 200 Danish kroner[12] into euros.

Few people, if any, notice that a woman is being deported right before their eyes. The officers provide Ann's identification documents to the pilot and watch her as she enters the plane and finds her seat at the back. She is being sent to Nigeria via Amsterdam. The officers and I remain standing there until the plane has left the gate and the wheels have lifted off. They call this an 'observed send-off'.

When I take a plane, I often look to see if there are passengers who are being deported. Sometimes they

[12] 23 GBP

are sitting between two plain-clothes officers, who rarely look very friendly. But people are not always deported on commercial flights. Sometimes, European countries charter a plane together to send a group of people back to Nigeria or other countries. Once I met a woman who was deported from the UK on a flight like that. On the way across Europe, the plane gathered more and more migrants, until there were about 150 of them on their way out of the EU. She told me, 'Sine, that was not a plane for tourists. It was just us and our guards. Some of us chatted as normal. Others cried, others were furious and others were silent. I didn't cry. I sat there feeling as if I were flying backwards through my life. We sat there in our seats and then we decided to throw ourselves from side to side inside the plane, to give the plane problems so it would have to turn around. But it didn't work.'

I don't know what happened to Ann after she left Denmark. This happens sometimes in migrant research. Most often, I do fieldwork alone, but in those periods where I follow the police, my contact with the migrants is brief and unpredictable. But after my experience with Ann's deportation, I feel even more strongly that I have to go to Nigeria. I need to know where Ann and the women I met in the interrogation rooms come from and what happens to them when they get deported.

Lagos

Lagos, Nigeria, 2011

'Dear Morten, Can you watch the kids in New York while I am doing fieldwork in Nigeria?'

Only a very accommodating ex-husband says yes to that kind of message. But Morten does. That winter, he arrives to be with the boys in New York, where they are going to school. I know they like being with their dad, but I am still a bit anxious when I say goodbye. This is my first trip to Nigeria, a land steeped in stories about danger. My new boyfriend, Janus, is going with me.

We land in Lagos in the middle of the night. The roof in the airport arrival hall is leaking and the room is filled with people dealing with their bags, suitcases and packages. The aroma of coffee and Nigerian food wafts in from the parking area outside, where people are grilling over open fires and where the long bright cones of vehicle headlights illuminate the dust from the sparsely paved roads.

Amid the noise, we find a taxi and are driven to our hotel for the days ahead. In the evening, there is a concert in the bar and it turns out to be a gathering place for the musicians, artists and journalists of Lagos. They are the creative class of the city, hanging out in a place that is 'upscale' compared to the impoverished neighbourhoods Janus and I will be wandering around in for the rest of our time here. We order large beers in 750 ml bottles, which we pour into glasses that have been in the freezer so ice forms on the outside. We eat chicken with piri-piri and chat with a Nigerian couple who normally live in London. They invite us to dinner with their friends the following evening. The magic of Nigeria begins to open to us.

The next day, we go to Jazzhole, a cool book and music shop, where the shelves are filled with Chimamanda Ngozi Adichie, Fela Kuti, Wole Soyinka and Chinua Achebe. It is impossible to see from the outside what a treasure trove is inside and how central a role the shop plays for music lovers and bookworms of Lagos. We eat tuna sandwiches and search for books about migration, sex work, gender and work, preferably written by Nigerians. There aren't many, but I buy what they have.

A television is on. Seal, the bestselling Nigerian-British singer, is dancing around in a music video. The man behind the counter looks up at the screen and says, 'I don't like him. After he got famous and married that model Heidi Klum, he forgot all about us, all about Nigeria. He never comes and plays concerts for us here. And we need that. Chimamanda is different. She practically lives here, she writes about us, she remembers us. You don't just leave and forget where you come from.'

The Get-Rich-Quick Syndrome

Along the road from the airport to Lagos stands a Catholic church with a metal roof and a cross painted on the gate. I have a meeting scheduled with its priest, Father Gabriel. At the entrance, there are two sacks containing clothing and rice, which neighbours have donated to the church. We sit by the priest's desk, between more sacks, while he speaks to us.

A few years ago, people started coming to this church straight from the airport. They were often tired and hungry, in worn clothing. They had been deported from Europe and let out from the airport's huge gates at the far end of the landing strip, where the deportation flights land. The people are let out, but to nothing. They wandered towards the city and people directed them to this church.

'I heard of people who were committing suicide by jumping off the motorway overpass into the city,' Gabriel says. 'So I decided to help these people who were returning home. I see them in the light of a lost son or daughter coming home.' He points at the small, framed painting behind him. A young man in trainers, a baseball cap and hoodie is standing with a lowered head as he is embraced by three men simultaneously, each one wearing clothing from the three largest tribes in Nigeria: Hausa, Yoruba and Igbo. Gabriel goes on, 'The ones who leave lose themselves in hopes of wealth. They sin, they sell sex, they commit crimes. But when they are deported, it is God's will that they return home to God, their father, their country and have their sins forgiven. I receive them here at the church with love. They get food, clothing and they call their families in the villages. But many of them will not return to their families. They are ashamed of being sent home. So they disappear into Lagos and try to get by. I don't always know where they end up.'

We talk about a situation in 1999, when a plane from Europe with deported sex workers landed at the international airport in Lagos for the first time. After their arrival, forty-seven women were put on display for ridicule and shaming by thirty million TV viewers. The Nigerian newspaper *The Post Express* wrote: '1999 was the year when Nigeria received the first blow against its image, when its female citizens were apprehended as prostitutes in Europe and deported.'[xi] This was one of the first times that news of Nigerian female sex workers in Europe reached the Nigerian public. While we sit in Gabriel's office, a copy of the photograph from *The Post Express* showing the deported women in the airport reminds me of the photo in *Ekstra Bladet* of the women in Vesterbro in handcuffs.

'Yes, they put the women on display and people were ashamed,' says Gabriel. 'It embarrasses us when Nigerians do things like that abroad. They travel to Europe, as if possessed by evil spirits that have given them the "get-rich-quick syndrome".'

'What do you mean?' I ask.

'We know a lot about slavery here in Nigeria. They sailed our brothers across the Atlantic Ocean from our coast right here.' Gabriel points towards the door, in the direction of the ocean. 'Slavery today,' he says, 'is not because people are forced onto ships and sailed away, like 300 years ago. Today, it is because people dream of a better life and easy money. They leave voluntarily, but end up as slaves.'

Mushin

'There is a woman from our church in Mushin who goes out to the brothels to help,' says Funlola. 'I will make a time for you to meet with her.' Funlola, a Nigerian, is my research assistant. I met her in New York, where we were both taking classes in the economic history of Africa. She uses all her personal contacts to give me access to the places relevant to my work.

Mushin is a poor, densely populated area of Lagos, where people come for the large, inexpensive markets selling food, leather and spare car parts. Crime in the area is brutal and the large number of men who come to do business also attracts sex workers.

After a few days, I meet Funlola's contact at the church, a large room inside a modern building. 'I go out to the brothels on Fridays,' she says, 'like today, and Saturdays. I talk with the women and invite them to the church on Sunday, so they can be blessed and receive free food. They don't often come, but I try.'

I follow her down the steps, out onto the street, past the food stalls. People stare at me. I obviously do not belong here.

The woman stops at a squat building and greets a couple of young men sitting outside. We go inside to a long, dim, concrete hallway with scratched turquoise walls and rooms on both sides. Most of the doors are open and my companion greets the young women who are sitting on mattresses on the floor in every room. Low light is emitted from the small string lights hung above the mattresses. The young women are wearing make-up and short dresses, with their hair done up. They are waiting for clients and they look up quickly as we come by. The woman tells them who I am and why I have come. 'The girls live in these rooms and here is where they receive their clients. They have between five and ten clients each day,' she tells me. 'They make three dollars per client,'[13] she says. 'If they have ten clients, that's thirty dollars. That is ten times what most people around here make in a day.'

She enters a room and sits on a mattress next to a girl whom she seems to know well. She tells her about my work and that I would like to talk with her and her girlfriends, if they have time. 'She would like to,' she tells me.

Most of the young women and girls I talk to at the brothel in Mushin have come here from rural areas looking for work. They knew that Mushin was a business centre and they hoped they could get work, despite job opportunities being scarce, even for those with degrees. Some of them were sent here by their parents to live with family members who didn't really take care of them, so they came to work at the brothel. They say they want to travel to Europe if they get the chance. But they don't have concrete travel plans yet. It seems overwhelming to imagine going from this little room in Mushin, at three dollars per client, to living in Europe. They say, 'I don't know how I would get there,' and 'It's too expensive.' They have not met anyone in Mushin who can help them get to Europe.

[13] 2 GBP

On Sunday, we are invited to the church to eat. Two of the women from the brothel are there. They are in their work clothes. They greet me, quickly eat the free food and leave before the service is over.

Roadblock

A few days later, we check out of our hotel in Lagos. The receptionist asks me where we are heading. 'Benin City,' I say.

'Did you know that they have black magic there and that Nigeria's prostitutes live there?' he replies. I nodded. 'Yes, I know,' I said.

Funlola and her husband pick us up and when we fill up the car with petrol before heading to Benin City, she folds her hands and prays that we will make it there and home safely.

The road leads us through the Nigerian rainforest for hours, down roads where the tarmac is washed away, leaving deep holes. Beside the road lie crumpled vehicles from accidents. Funlola says that rural people are fighting to make the government and local authorities pay for tarmac and safe roads. Many people lose their lives in needless accidents and it takes a long time for people to reach the city to sell their goods.

We are listening to Nigerian pop music and Funlola is telling us all about her country – about the difference between the north and the south, about the politics and about Nollywood, the thriving film industry. Suddenly, the car stops and my seatbelt tightens across my chest. In front of us, we see thick, wooden poles across the road and a group of men in orange vests with automatic rifles waves us to the side.

'You have not paid to pass,' says one of them, leaning through Funlola's passenger window. He stares at

Janus and me, and I want to say, 'Hey, I have two kids back home. Please don't do anything to us.'

Funlola's husband raises his voice. 'We do not have to pay anything and you know that very well. Just because we have two foreign passengers, we are not from an oil company or something. They are our guests here in Nigeria. Go tell your boss that.' He nods in the direction of a man standing at a distance, who looks like the boss.

'But you have to pay. That's how it is when you cross a state line,' says the young man.

Funlola's husband is getting angry now. 'No, we don't. Stop bothering peaceful people. Go over to your boss.'

I think that he has obviously done this before and I feel a bit calmer, even though I am still nervous that he will get into trouble because of us.

'Just pay, so we can go,' says Funlola, anxiously but firmly.

'No, I won't. Just because they have guns. It gives Nigeria a bad name and if I pay, they will keep doing it.'

The young man returns to our car. He has spoken with his boss. 'You can go,' he says, a bit defeated. They move the poles and wave us past. We sit in sweaty silence.

Benin City

As we drive into Benin City, the connections to Europe are obvious. One shop is called Little Italy Plaza. One hotel is called Torino. Signs offer language classes in Spanish, Italian and Swedish. We drive past a huge billboard featuring a picture of a boat about to sink in the Mediterranean, alongside corpses lying desiccated in the Saharan sand. The slogan reads: DON'T TRAVEL – THE DESERT AND THE SEA ARE DANGEROUS – STAY HOME. On another billboard, a woman in a short skirt and red stiletto heels is leaning through a car window, flirting with a customer. Beneath the picture, it reads: WOMAN, STAY HOME – YOU CAN BECOME A VICTIM OF TRAFFICKING AND PROSTITUTION. There is no suggestion about what the woman could do instead.

Benin City stands out on the map of the global sex industry and that is not a coincidence. It is the capital of Edo State, which borders the Niger Delta, has always been in contact with Europe through the slave trade, oil, lumber, copper and rubber. Now, migrants follow those same routes. At the end of the 1980s, a new group of Europeans started arriving in Benin City due to the economic opportunities available, especially Italian companies. Some of these Italian men married Nigerian women and brought them back to Italy. At the same time, there was a big demand for workers in Italy, especially agricultural workers. Some of the women who had moved

Anti-trafficking billboards outside of Benin City, Nigeria

Becky shows the author where she wants to go: Europe

to Italy with their husbands established themselves as so-called 'madams', helping others travel to Europe, legally at first. But as Europe tightened its visa regulations and 'Fortress Europe' began taking shape after the Treaty of Amsterdam in 1997, the madams arranged illegal and dangerous routes, with human smugglers as the middlemen. Migration to Europe became a way to make money, both for the women who were in Europe already, and for all of the middlemen arranging the journey across the Sahara Desert via Niger to Libya. Some women were approached and recruited with tempting questions: 'Do you want to go to Europe? We can help you.' But most migrants sought the traffickers out themselves, because they saw no alternatives in Nigeria.

The women who wanted to go to Europe were often too poor to pay for the journey, so they went into debt to be able to travel. They would have to repay their debt by selling sex when they reached their destinations. The harder it was to reach Europe, the higher the cost. At the start, many of them did not know what kind of work awaited them. But today, almost all of them do, because they have family members who made the journey before them, who have told them how Nigerian women earn money in Europe. Also, there are public information posters, such as the ones I saw in Benin City, and various organisations hold educational events in the smaller villages.

But none of this keeps the women from going. In 2016, approximately 11,000 Nigerian women travelled to Europe, the greatest number on record.[xii] This number fluctuates, but there is no indication that the desire to leave is decreasing. Benin City receives the largest amount of money sent back to Nigeria from migrants in Europe, and the city has had the greatest increase in construction projects paid for by migrant women.[xiii]

Armed Robbers

We are going to stay with some of Funlola's distant relatives. She has not seen them in decades, but they receive us warmly in their second-floor apartment on the edge of the city. The table is set with roasted chicken and jollof rice – spiced rice with tomato, onion and red pepper. A single fan turns above us on the ceiling. The TV is on, airing one of the popular soap operas from Nollywood, and the family's two teenagers are hanging out on the sofa. Their parents sit with us at the table and tell us about Benin City and their life here. The mother is a housewife, while the father drives every morning to the school where he works. They hope to place their children in the university in Abuja and maybe after that send them to study in London.

I tell them a bit about my work and why I am in Benin City; that I am researching why and how women leave and what happens when they are deported back to Nigeria. The mother says, 'A lot of women who were sent back home live right down the road from here. You can come with me and meet Chika, our neighbour's daughter. She was in Italy and, further down the road, there is one who left and I think she's still in Italy.'

After we eat, she shows us around the apartment. Janus and I have a bedroom with a bed and a closet. A light blue curtain flaps in the open window. 'Lock the door and shut the window at night,' says the mother. 'We lock the bars in front of the entry door and we lock the gate in the yard. We had an armed robbery recently. They hit my husband and my son in the face and took my husband's new watch. We didn't really have anything else of value. But my husband got a gash on his face.' I can see that this was terribly upsetting for her and I feel a twinge of anxiety. I reassure her, 'Yes, we will lock the door.'

The next morning, we have toast, tea and sliced bananas for breakfast. I follow the mother to her neighbour's house along the dusty red road. In front of a small brown house, an elderly woman is sitting under a yellow parasol, selling bananas from a cart. Our host says, 'Is Chika home? My guest would like to meet her.' It turns out that the banana seller is Chika's mother. She points at the door. 'She's in there,' she says, smiling at me with an air of curiosity.

Chika comes out and says hello. She appears to be in her thirties, with a friendly face, straightened black hair, a white T-shirt and a flowing, flowery skirt. She has a prominent round scar on the bridge of her nose.

I tell her that I would like to know where she has been in Italy and I explain why I am in Benin City. I ask if she would like to tell me her story. 'Come inside,' she says. In the hot living room with red-painted walls, Chika's grandmother is sitting on the sofa watching a soap opera. Chika takes a bottle of water from the fridge and offers it to me. 'There are a lot of us in the area who were sent back home,' she says. 'They would probably like to talk to you too.

'I waited such a long time to be able to stay in Italy,' she continues. 'I tried everything. I wanted to stay there because I had left my two children here with my mother and I sent money home to them. They were going to a good school and everything was better. But after I was sent home, I had to take them out of school, so now here I am, dependent on my mother's money.'

She looks over at her grandmother, who is listening and nodding.

'A man from the Albanian mafia gave me this,' she says, pointing at her nose. 'In a way, that started my getting sent home. It was in Torino. I was raped by five men while I was working in a deserted area. One of them pushed a hot pistol against my nose and told me to be quiet. I was found later, in a field, by someone walking a dog. They said I was nearly dead. An Italian woman really tried to help me and found me a lawyer. The Italians said I was a victim of trafficking and I told the police everything I knew about the people I owed money to in Nigeria and about the men who had raped me. I thought that would help, but even though I told them everything, they still sent me home.'

'Did anyone help you when you were sent home?'

'I was promised some money from Italy, because they thought I was a trafficking victim. But the money didn't arrive for six months. I had to borrow money to survive until then. When the money came, I bought cooking pots, plastic chairs, food and opened a little food cart just outside the city at a rest area, where truck drivers and sex workers who work at the rest area bought food from me. The cart was going really well. But late one evening, two armed robbers came and stole all my money and my pots.'

Chika's mother comes inside and sits next to the grandmother. They listen while Chika keeps talking. I ask if we should go into another room. 'No,' she says. 'They know everything. They are hoping I can travel back to Europe, but now I want to stay home with my children. They are growing and they need me. But I am a grown woman. I don't want to live here with my mother. I hope I can find a place for me and my children.'

Outside the window, I can hear shouting, loud talking and laughter as someone approaches the house. Then two women appear in the doorway. 'They said you had white guests. I wanted to stop in!' says one of the women to Chika. She is wearing a colourful batik shirt and happily dancing and shouting to the music from the TV, as if she just arrived at a party. 'Here is where it's happening; here, here is where it's happening,' she sings and dances around, while laughing hoarsely. She has a lively face, hair dyed two colours and big, round earrings. I love her energy from the moment she walks into the room.

Chika introduces us. 'This is Sine. She is from Europe and she wants to talk about it with us who live in Benin City. Sine, Becky wants to travel to Europe, don't you, Becky?'

'Yes, I want to go to Italy, I want to go to Italy,' she more or less sings. 'I have tried, actually.' She calms down a bit. 'But it didn't work out and I had to turn around.' She clicks her tongue in regret as she sits on the sofa.

I have the sense that there is much more to that story and I ask if she will meet with me another day and tell me more. 'Sure, we can do that. But I already told you, didn't I?'

'I know, but I would like to know more about it.'

'OK, we can do that.' She gets up from the sofa. 'Hey, Chika, let's have our pictures taken with Sine.' Chika gets up. Becky poses like a professional. She sticks out her behind and dances with Chika. I kiss her on the cheek. I have a series of photos from the first day I met Becky. One of them is stuck on my fridge in Vesterbro.

Becky

Becky calls herself a 'zipped-lip girl' – a woman, as she describes herself, who doesn't say anything to anyone, because that is the best way to protect oneself. But she is happy to tell me about her life. She says, 'You aren't dangerous.'

We meet frequently at her aunt's house, where she lives with her aunt's three small children in two narrow rooms. They share a bath and a toilet with a female neighbour and her children. In the tamped-earth courtyard between the two low buildings stands a clothes-drying rack, plastic tubs for laundry and a large wooden mortar for crushing cassava root into white, gelatinous fufu porridge. Becky's aunt often sits on a green plastic chair in the yard nursing her baby while we are inside the house, where Becky prepares food for her family in two large pots on a gas burner. Chilli peppers, spinach, onion, tomato paste and a stock cube. Occasionally, she adds a small amount of beef or chicken. We spend many afternoons like this; Becky telling me her story amid the pots and the spreading aromas, while I sit on a low chair in the kitchen, rinsing vegetables.

'I don't have a real job right now, but several boyfriends give me money. That is why I am here in Benin City. It is easier to get by as a single girl.'

Becky grew up in a Muslim family in Adamawa State in northern Nigeria, not far from the region where the jihadist groups Boko Haram wreak havoc.

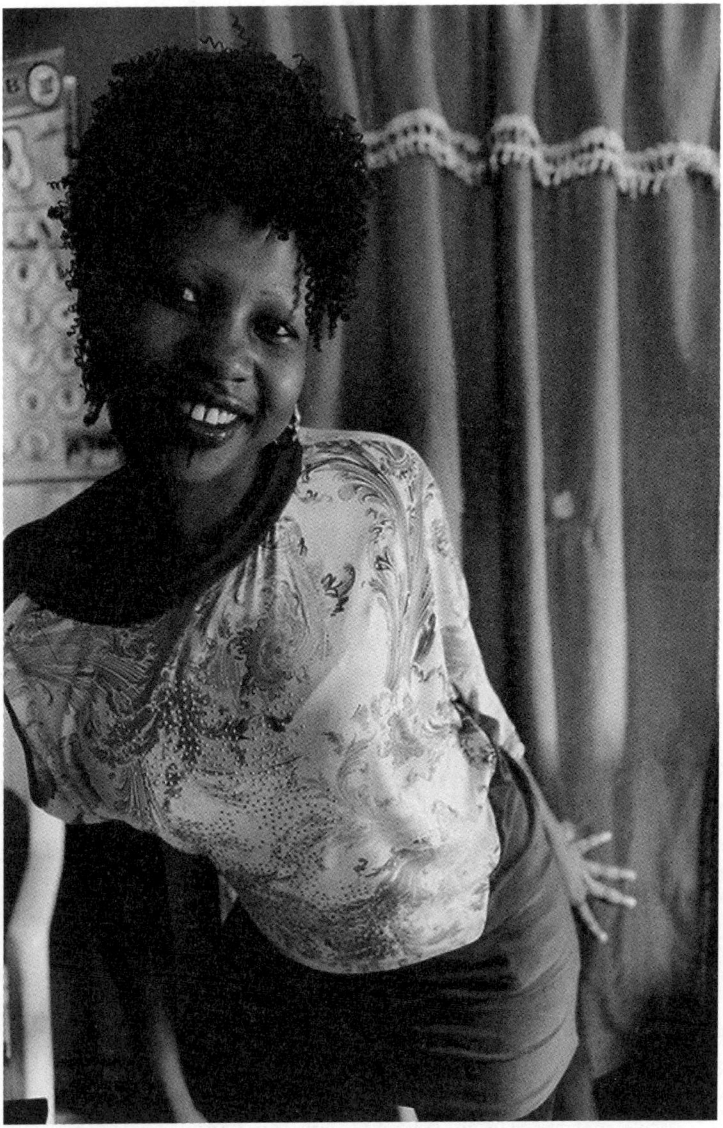

Becky

Boko Haram is part of the global radical jihadist movement and has terrorised mostly the northern regions leaving a trail of sorrow, tears and blood in its wake. It targets churches and mosques, Christians and Muslims, civilians and uniformed personnel. It was behind the bombing of the United Nations headquarters in Abuja in 2011, media headquarters and many police stations. It is estimated that more than 20,000 people have been killed by Boko Haram since 2009, but the actual numbers are likely to be higher.[xiv]

The situation for girls and young women in northern Nigeria is one of the reasons that Becky left for the south and the more Christian Benin City. Her family refused to meet her non-Muslim boyfriends, and she wanted to decide for herself who she dated.

Before she tried to go to Europe for the first time, Becky converted from Islam to Christianity. 'I converted because Muslim women don't travel to Europe and do what I am going to do in Italy. It's a sin. But, you know, the good thing about the Christian God, compared to Allah and the African gods, who punish you right away, is that He forgives all your sins. When you turn back to God, he forgives you. Being Christian works well for me, because I have to put God on standby once in a while in my life and do what I have to. Otherwise, I wouldn't survive.'

Becky enrolled at a respected media school in Jos for about a year, but she didn't like it. She dreamed of something else, something bigger. 'I got some money from my father to go to school, but I spent it on a visa and a ticket to Italy. Or I thought I did. I got all the way to the airport in Lagos, but they could see that my documents were false and the police stopped me and said that I was on my way to Europe to sell sex. That

I had been tricked by the people who send others to Europe. I felt so dumb. I couldn't tell my father that I spent the school money on that. My plan was to make it to Europe and surprise everyone. I would work and send money home. It didn't work out that way. I tried again later, over land, but that failed too. So now I am dreaming about trying again. The people I have met who have been in Europe, oh my God, they look so beautiful when they come back to Nigeria to visit. Gorgeous hair and nails. If I get the chance, I will go. Today, tomorrow, any time.'

Built-in ATM

One afternoon, we are sitting in Becky's aunt's house, drinking Lipton tea with sugar cubes and eating sliced bananas that Becky bought at the market. We are watching Nigerian music videos on local TV. Between two videos, there is a public-service warning in yellow letters on a green sign: SAY NO TO PROSTITUTION. DON'T GO TO EUROPE.

I say to Becky, 'I have seen all these signs hanging around Benin City, warning women not to go to Europe because they can become victims of trafficking. What do you think of them?'

'Of course I've seen them,' she says. 'Everyone knows what the women do in Italy. The madam who could help me get to Italy has told me that she doesn't have any real work for me, or us, just prostitution. And I would have to walk the streets every day. I know that if I don't want to work as a prostitute, then there is no reason to go to Europe. No one is putting a gun to our heads and forcing us to go. So I don't believe in trafficking. That's just a word white people have invented. Travelling to Europe is a deal between parties: the woman, her family and her madam. We negotiate a deal that all parties agree to ... Those signs don't do a thing.'

'Don't you think they might convince some people?' I ask.

'Maybe they have an impact on some people, but I don't know anyone who pays attention to them. Chika knew what could happen and she went anyway. You don't stay here because of a sign.

'It's because they don't want us going to Europe. They don't want us there. And the rich Nigerians don't want us to improve our lives. We know it's dangerous, but we don't want to stay here. There is no work and so many are leaving. Everyone knows someone who went. Besides, God has forgotten about Nigeria. Our leaders gobble up our money. Nigeria's economy is bad. No one is taking care of us, so we have to take care of ourselves . . .' With a hoarse laugh, Becky says, 'My solution is the woman's built-in ATM.'

This is Becky's Story

A couple of days later, I hand out six new notebooks and blue pens to Becky and five other women. I have brought the blank books with me from Denmark. The women stand there, paging through them and clicking the pens.

'You can write whatever you want in the books,' I tell them. 'If you write something about your trip to Europe and what it was like to return to Nigeria, or your plans about leaving again, that would be great. But even if you just write about what your normal days are like over the next couple of weeks, I would learn a lot from that too.'

'I think I will ask my daughter to help me,' says one of the women. 'She is a lot better at writing than I am. Is that OK?'

'Sure, that's fine.'

They return the journals to me with descriptions of their lives in their own words. Some of them wrote one page, some a bit more. They wrote mostly about their travels, their time on the street and their plans to return to Europe. And then about their children and about their lack of work and money.

At the top of the page in Becky's book, she wrote, 'This is Becky's story'. Below is what she wrote about her second attempt to reach Europe.

> I went to Libya because Nigeria's economy is so bad. I went over land, which is the most dangerous route.

But I didn't have any other options. I went across the desert to Libya and my mother did not know that I left.

We took a bus from Benin to Kano and from Kano to Katsina and from Katsina, we rode motorcycles to cross the border between Nigeria and Niger. We made it over the border, but in Niger, they arrested all of us and put us in prison. Then the man who brought us to Libya gave the police some money, so they let us go.

My first day in the Sahara Desert was fun. We were happy to have left Nigeria. That's how I felt at first. At six in the evening, the driver stopped the truck and said it was time to make some food. We started, but at 6.30 he said, 'Ahya.' That meant 'Onwards'. We had to leave again and the food wasn't even done. We ate it raw.

On the second day, we were still driving. We got washed at four in the morning, because the weather was so hot and because there are sicknesses in the desert. If you don't get washed by four o'clock, you can get a sickness that makes your throat twist up until you die. That's how it goes.

On the third day, I asked the driver if we would be in Libya soon. He said no. That we had barely even started.

On the fifth day, there was no more food or water. So I went over to the other truck. Every time we stopped, I went over to the other truck and ate with those passengers. That is how I survived to get to Libya. Above us, the sun was fucking hot.

After being in the desert for two weeks, I knew that nothing in this life comes easy. I started to cry to Dave, the one who was taking me to Libya. I cried and said, 'Where are you taking me?' He said, 'Libya. It's OK, Becky. You will be there soon.'

After three weeks in the desert, I finally arrived in Libya. Libya is beautiful. I like it there, but Libyan men scare me. They are bad. They screw Nigerian girls without using condoms. If the Libyan police catch you with a condom, you get arrested for prostitution. They lock you in a cell. Libya is nice, but there is no freedom. We stayed inside the whole time, especially us girls. We had no freedom.

We broke off pieces of foam from the mattresses on the floor and put them in our vaginas so we wouldn't get pregnant.

The woman who was helping me get to Italy wired some money to Dave, so he could pay for my trip over the sea to Italy. I mean the Mediterranean. Dave paid and they moved me to Zuwara, a city on the coast.

When I finally saw the ocean, I prayed to God that he would close the ocean. It was so huge and noisy. I was scared.

Then it happened. Two days before I was supposed to leave, the military closed the ocean. They said we had to go back where we came from, back to our home country. They said we couldn't cross into Italy, and our journey back home started. Back through the desert again.

My girlfriend Maria was in the bed of the truck on the way back. She was nine months pregnant. I thought, Oh God, what if she goes into labour? What should I do? I had no idea that was exactly what was about to happen. She gave birth in the desert three days later. When she went into labour, I didn't know how to help a woman give birth. But I was the doctor that day. I did whatever I could.

I had heard that the mother could put a teaspoon in her mouth to help push out the placenta. I said *push, push*, just like I had seen on TV. But in the end, she stopped pushing, because the placenta wouldn't come out. And she kept bleeding.

The baby came out, but Maria died. I didn't know what to do. I cried. I took her beautiful baby, who was half white; the father was Libyan. I took some water from the canteen and gave the baby a bath. Then I found an envelope of milk powder like you use in coffee and I mixed it with water. I gave it to the baby and swaddled it in clothes. When we arrived in the desert city of Agadez, I gave the baby to Dave. But he gave the baby back to me and said it was mine now!

So I took the baby with me to the market and bought some milk. I didn't really have any money. I braided hair for people and made a little for myself and the baby. We finally made it to Nigeria and I called the baby's grandmother, the mother of my dead friend.

When we arrived in Benin City, I took the baby to his grandmother. She asked us about her daughter. I told her that we left her in Libya and that she gave us her baby to bring back to her.

The grandmother took the baby. She said that since her daughter was in Libya and she had given us the baby, that meant that she would return. She never found out that her daughter died giving birth. I was afraid that she would blame me. My dear girlfriend died on the way home and I buried her in the desert. I came back without her.

Kidnapping

When Becky drops off her notebook, she suggests that we go with Chika to the neighbourhood chicken restaurant. Funlola had recommended that we not eat at the local restaurants, only at the pizzeria or the chicken restaurant next to the police station. But it seems OK to go to this place.

At the entrance to the restaurant, I see three young men sitting at a table, with large beers in dark bottles and roasted chicken in front of them. They glance at me and I sense that they say something about me among themselves. I remind myself about my decision not to get nervous when I get an unsafe feeling here in Benin City, otherwise it would be impossible to work here.

Funlola's husband had to return to Lagos, so she has hired Mike, a family friend, to drive us around Benin City in an old brown Mercedes from the 1980s, with worn seats and open windows. It is one of the cars that was sold to Nigeria after exhausting its usefulness in Germany. Funlola explained that it is best not to have a car that looks expensive here. We don't want to signal that there is any reason to rob us. We have to blend in as much as possible and there are parts of Benin City where we will need a driver who knows the areas we should avoid or drive through without stopping. Before we arrived in Benin City, Funlola told me, 'In Nigeria, everything goes good, until suddenly it doesn't.'

Mike is a friendly older man who often prefers to

eat in the car, so he can keep an eye on it. I order chicken and jollof rice and fried ripe bananas. Becky and Chika order the same thing. We sit at a table. Today, Mike is sitting at the furthest table from us, from which he can see the car.

I watch the three men leave the restaurant and I think that the brief tinge of fear that I felt was an embarrassing reminder of the brain's prejudice, now proven wrong. We chat at our table while we wait for our food. Chika's phone rings and she stands up and walks towards the door and the car park. A minute passes.

Suddenly, she comes running back into the restaurant and yells in panic, 'We need to run out to the car NOW!' I don't know what has scared Chika so much, but we grab our bags and run.

We race down the five steps to where Mike's Mercedes is waiting with the doors open and the motor running. Chika more or less pushes us all inside on top of each other, slams the door and gets in next to Mike. She yells, 'Drive!' He speeds out of the car park into the busy street without stopping and weaves in and out of cars at full speed. Chika says, 'Keep your heads down!'

My heart is pounding in my chest and I finally ask what is going on. Chika says, 'Mike tailed the three strange guys who were in the corner of the restaurant when we got there. Did you see them?'

'I definitely saw them,' I say.

'Mike had a bad feeling about them right away, so when they left the restaurant, he followed them. They didn't know he was with us, since he was sitting by himself. He stood right behind one of the guys and heard him say on the phone, "Hurry over here. There are white people and a job to do." That's how kidnapping happens. Someone sees some rich people, or white people, and they call some others. They get some of the ransom money for notifying them. Their friends could have been there in two seconds with weapons and made you get into their car. Generally, bystanders are shocked and don't do anything. We knew we had to act fast.'

'OK,' I say, 'so we were almost kidnapped?'

Chika replies, 'Yes, I'm pretty sure of that.'

Back at the hotel, I am filled with adrenaline and worry. I have never felt as afraid as I felt in the backseat of Mike's Mercedes while we tore through the streets, not knowing if we were actually in danger of being kidnapped. We had been totally helpless and completely dependent on Chika, Mike and Becky. These women, who often are described as vulnerable victims, saved us.

I call home to Julius and Carl to hear their voices.

Europe is Real

Benin City, 2012

The next year, I fly back to Nigeria. I am now five months pregnant with Ella, my third child, my first with Janus. Before Ella arrives, I want to do a last round of fieldwork in Nigeria, so I can complete my PhD. I rumble over the Sahara Desert on a turbulent flight and land in the intensely hot airport, where Busayo, my new research assistant and friend, picks me up. He looks at my belly when I come out with my baggage and says, 'We will have to pretend that you are my wife. Otherwise, people will think you are crazy to be in Nigeria alone and pregnant without your husband.' So the 'married couple', Busayo and Sine, walk out to the car park.

There have been quite a few kidnappings and armed robberies in the neighbourhood where we lived last year, where the women live. Busayo thinks it is safer for me to live in the city centre, so I rent a small hotel room across from the police station. There are guards with AK-47s when we drive into the car park and there is barbed wire atop the high walls surrounding the hotel complex. It is hard for me to tell if it is necessary or exaggerated worry. But I follow Busayo's advice.

Becky comes over the next morning with a bag of fruit she bought at the market. She also has a bag of clothes. She ends up living in my room for several weeks, where she can sit in my air conditioning, watch cable TV and drink spring water. One day, while I'm out, she eats all the chocolate I brought with me from Denmark, meant for the late-night hours when I am writing my notes.

'Yes, I ate all of it,' she admits, flatly. 'I love your chocolate. It's real. Everything in Nigeria is fake. I also love the shoes my aunt in Italy sent to me. They're real. That's why I love Europe. Europe is real.'

One evening, Becky wants to try the city's only pizzeria, which is right across from my hotel. She takes me firmly by the arm and we cross the darkened street, which is only illuminated by the cars' headlights. With its modern facade of layered, polished glass and blinding light pouring out, the pizzeria is like a shining diamond in the centre of its dark car park. It has an air-conditioned interior, music, bright white tile floors, a play area for children and a menu with plain, pepperoni and Sicilian pizza. 'I love this place,' says Becky. 'I want to try a gelato for dessert.' We order and sit down.

Becky called Chika beforehand and asked if she wanted to join us. When she arrives, she says, 'Oh, I miss pizza and gelato.' She's wearing a leather cap, large earrings, tight pants and high heels. She did herself up to go out for pizza.

'This pizza doesn't taste like the kind in Italy,' she says with disappointment. She has a large pepperoni pizza in front of her. 'It's just a Nigerian version.'

'What is the Italian kind like?' Becky asks her.

'It has more cheese and the tomato sauce doesn't taste like chilli peppers, and the crust isn't damp,' says Chika, putting a slice on her plate. 'That's what I miss about Italy. Pizza, ice cream and a comfortable life.'

'What do you mean by a comfortable life?' I ask.

One of Becky's Facebook posts

'Italy is nothing like this,' she says. 'They have electricity, air conditioning, toilets and things work. Life is so difficult here in Nigeria.'

A younger woman nears our table with a mop. Suddenly, Chika says, 'Hi,' and the woman says 'Hi,' back, surprised. The two know each other. 'So you're back from Italy too?' asks Chika.

'Yes,' says the woman. 'They sent me home a few months ago. Now I have this cleaning job.'

Chika turns towards me. Becky is listening closely. 'We met in Italy. We walked the streets together there, but we haven't seen each other since then.'

Chika asks her, 'Did you get any help from Italy when you were sent home?'

'They promised me some,' she says, 'but I haven't seen any money yet. So I'm working here. I want to go back to Italy.'

Chika nods. 'I got some money after a long wait. Then I started a food cart, but I got robbed.'

The woman keeps mopping the floor. Becky is lost in thought as she eats her gelato.

Do You Know What's Going on Here?

One afternoon, a few days later, I get into Mike's old brown Mercedes, which Busayo and I are travelling around in. We drive to a secret location on the outskirts of Benin City and park in front of a row of nondescript buildings. This is where the women who were captured in dustpan manoeuvres, brothel raids or otherwise taken by authorities in Europe and deported to Benin City live. These are women whom the authorities believe were victims of trafficking. I have a meeting scheduled with the manager of the place.

We are let in through a high gate that slams hard behind us. The manager is Nigerian; friendly and insightful as she shows me around and asks me about the situation for Nigerian women in Denmark and what the laws are like. The buildings here are newly painted and well-trained pink roses climb the walls. There are mini-vans parked in the tidy courtyard, on which are written in discreet black lettering 'Donated by Italy' and 'Donated by Holland'. The place exudes European money.

The manager says, 'Come meet some of the girls.' We walk past several empty rooms, where there are made-up beds and children's beds with teddy bears on them. 'We don't get that many here,' she says when I ask why the rooms are empty. 'They don't want to live here when they get sent home. Some of them return to their families, but most try to go abroad again.'

In the TV room, there are three young women. Two of them are sitting on a sofa; one is braiding the other's hair. They appear to be in their early twenties. The manager says to one of the other employees, 'Let's get this cleaned up,' and to me, 'A foreign delegation is arriving soon, so we have to make it look neat. You can sit and chat with these girls. They were just sent back from Russia.'

I sit down. One girl asks me, 'Where are you from?' They all seem eager to talk, as if they were sitting here bored, hoping something would happen.

'I'm from Denmark. I am visiting Benin City for a little while, because a lot of women from Nigeria are coming to my country. So I travelled here to find out why, and what happens when they get sent back to Nigeria again.'

One of them says, 'I wasn't in Russia as long as I wanted to be. I was in Moscow, but they caught me and sent me home. Now I have been here for three weeks and they won't let me leave and go home to my mother, because they think my trafficker will come and take me away again. They took my telephone, so I can't call my mother.'

The two young women trade places on the sofa and keep braiding.

'They say that they have to catch my trafficker before I can go home. But I'm not afraid. It's just someone we borrowed money from, someone my parents know. I want to leave again, so I can keep paying off the debt, and my madam would rather have me pay off my debt too, instead of sitting here in Benin City. So if I get out, she can help me leave again.'

The young women stand up and ask if I want to eat with them. We walk to the kitchen, where they make their own food. We eat spinach stew and fufu. After we eat, they talk with a staff member about their experiences in Russia. I think it is a kind of therapy.

I sit at the kitchen table and write in my notebook with my back to the door. Suddenly, I hear a deep male voice behind me. 'Excuse me, could you help me with what's going on here?' I turn around and see a tall white man with blond hair, wearing a light blue shirt. He looks like a diplomat. He walks over and presents himself. 'I have come from Holland to see the anti-trafficking projects we have given money to. We are only here in Benin City for three hours and then we are going to Abuja. But it is difficult to find out what is happening. There are no women here at the centre. We thought it would be filled with all the Nigerian women we see on the streets of Amsterdam, after all the money we sent down here.'

'I also just arrived here this morning,' I say. 'That is, I have been in Benin City for a while. But I think it's better if you talk with the manager of this place instead of me. She is very knowledgeable.'

'OK,' he says. 'I just thought that maybe since you were from Europe, you could help us to understand what is happening here.'

'Sorry, I can't help you. I hope you figure it out. Nice to meet you.' I turn back to my notebook. He leaves and walks out to the courtyard.

Later in the afternoon, I say goodbye to the three women, who are now sitting on the veranda in front of the house, drinking water and looking bored. We shake hands and they wave goodbye.

I hear some shouts and complaints from a house with barred windows in one corner of the courtyard. 'That is one of the women we think might be a trafficker,' explains the manager. 'Sometimes we get women and we are not sure if they are victims of trafficking or if they were helping women get to Europe. They can't live with the others, so they live over there until we can investigate the situation.'

'I want to speak to someone!' yells the woman. 'I will not stay here!' A staff member goes to the barred window and speaks with the woman inside. I think about Sonia, with the rivets on her white leggings, whom we raced around to catch on Istedgade. And about Ann, whom we drove to the deportation flight. Everything changes when you stand here, looking towards Europe.

That evening, Becky and her friends come to the hotel bar. They want to drink beer and watch the Champions League on the hotel's large television. We eat chicken with jollof rice and my baby kicks when the fans shout and cheer for Manchester United. 'Feel the baby kick,' I say to Becky. She is the first person besides me to feel the baby, who has only started kicking since I arrived in Nigeria. Becky orders me a Guinness. 'You have to drink dark beer,' she says, making fists and kicking movements with her hands. 'It makes the baby strong and kick even more.'

There is Nothing God Cannot Do

Becky and I are sitting next to each other on dark red metal chairs in the airport, waiting for my connecting flight to Lagos. I am flying back to Denmark to visit my mother in Viborg before returning to Janus and the boys in New York City. When I landed in Benin City, they were playing Dolly Parton and Kenny Rogers singing 'Islands in the Stream' and it is still playing now. The song feels too romantic for this place, as if it is intended to calm people's nerves. There are not many waiting, just a small group of Chinese men and me. That is how it is every time I land or take off from here. It is a small airport with an entrance, an exit and two little shops selling books, newspapers, drinks and sweets. About twenty guards stand outside holding Kalashnikov rifles.

I walk up to the counter and check in, buy water and a fizzy drink for Becky. She says softly, 'I was watching you stand over there with your baby in your belly. I hope we will meet again.' I hug her with my pregnant belly between us. We say that if she ever does come to Europe, we will eat ice cream with my kids in Copenhagen on a summer's day.

Soon I make my way to the aeroplane. 'Are you travelling alone?' asks a friendly steward, glancing at my round belly. He sits me in business class, even though I have an economy ticket. I am the only person in the section. He brings me apple juice and a newspaper.

The plane shakes violently when we take off and

I look down at Benin City's little airport building with Becky inside, and at the enormous forest we fly over on the way to Lagos. In a few places, columns of smoke rise through the canopy.

When I arrive in Viborg, my mother is standing in the doorway of her house on her residential street. The winter sun is in her face and her cheekbones protrude sharply, maybe because her hair is back in a ponytail.

'Have you lost weight, Mum?' I ask.

'Yes, I have, but it's just because I stopped eating cake at work. And I go swimming on Tuesdays.'

We spend a few days together, filled with talk of my fieldwork, the baby in my belly and her grandchildren in New York. She is relieved that I am finished with travelling to Nigeria. She has gifts for the kids. She is always finding gadgets, sewing things, finding things in second-hand shops for me and for them. We hug goodbye over my round belly and, again, I notice her thin arms. But I don't say anything. We already talked about why she got thinner. She gets tears in her eyes, like she always does when I leave. We decide that she will come to New York and watch the boys when I'm ready to give birth.

In April, she gets a terrible stomach-ache. She doesn't think she can come to New York and be there at the birth. I feel lonely without her presence and care. We write to each other on 2 May. Then the emails and texts stop. I am in week thirty-six. The doctors say that she has terminal colon cancer and that she won't live long. Maybe a few months. It takes five weeks.

I've never felt such horrible heaviness in my whole life. It is unbelievable. I am too pregnant to travel; I have to give birth before I can return home and see my mother die. My midwife in New York cries when I tell her, because she just lost her husband to cancer. Her expression is firm and friendly and she puts her arms around me. Her hands are warm and coarse.

On 15 April, Becky wrote from Benin City, 'How's it going? I can't wait to see your beautiful baby. Remember to rest. I am looking for a pretty name for your baby.'

On 8 May, I respond, 'Thank you for looking for a name. I just found out that my mother has cancer in her belly. I love her so much, so that is very difficult. Love, Sine.'

Becky answers right away. 'I am so sorry, Sine. Don't worry. Your mother will get well again. I know that my God will make her healthy. There is nothing God can't do. I will keep praying. I love you. Take care.'

Ghost Mothers

New York City and Viborg, 2012

Ella's birth is very bloody, more so than normal. 'You never know with the third child,' says my midwife. I had considered a home birth, but it was good I decided against it. As if through a fog, I see the doctor shake his head, rush me to the operating room and stop my bleeding while Janus is left abandoned in the birthing room with little Ella in his arms and my bloody flip-flops on the floor.

The next day, Ella is lying beside me in the Brooklyn hospital bed, swathed in a blue and pink hospital gown, a cosy little package. I call my mother. She is tired and speaks in a whisper. I want her to be my mother, with a strong voice, but she is 6,000 kilometres away and her voice is nearly inaudible. Neither she, my father nor my siblings had told me the extent of her illness. She has been protecting me and I have also been protecting myself, so I could give birth while she was dying. But now I need her hand, with its soft, warm, weathered veins, which I pressed on as a child when we held hands. Her words, though they could sometimes be stern, were there to support me. I am an adult woman who wants her mother, but I can't reach her any more.

We leave for Denmark almost immediately, with an emergency passport for Ella. Our insurance company puts me in business class with my newborn daughter, six days old. She lies on my belly all the way across the

Atlantic. I lost a lot of blood during the birth and the doctors were not sure if I should fly.

In the car on the way to Viborg, I'm afraid of seeing my mother in a hospital bed, at home in her living room. I hear her scream when we come in the door. She knows that it's me, coming to say goodbye. Her scream is long, sad and eerie. When I see her, it is as if it is not her lying in the living room, but someone else. There is an old woman with parchment-like skin over protruding bones. She can hardly talk and she cries quietly. Incredibly tired, and full of morphine, she lies there while my sister dabs her lips occasionally with a piece of damp cottonwool. While we sit with her, she whispers, 'I am going to die. That is what I have to do. I have to say goodbye.' We lay Ella on her bed and place my mother's thin gray hand on her belly. She pats her gently with a sense of finality.

Over the next two days, the air of the living room feels increasingly thick and heavy. Every breath from my mother sounds like a long sigh. Her pulse is getting weaker. I can see it on her neck. And every time it pulsates under her thin skin, it moves one beat closer to the inevitable. We are gathered around her sickbed. The nurse says that her organs are slowly shutting down. This is what she will die from. Finally, with a raspy gasp, her breathing stops. We look at the artery on her neck. It has stopped too.

Time stands still. That's how it feels, and that's what happens. We close the little clock on her bedside table as a sign that her time has stopped. My mother. She isn't here any more. We open a window, hoping that her soul will find its way out, even though we want her to stay with us. Her warm pillow gets passed around after she dies, with the warmth of her body still inside. This is the last of her we can hold.

I still can't fathom that I watched my mother die. That it really happened. That death happens. There was so much she thought she still had to do. Things she had saved for all the years she thought were ahead of her. She was only sixty-one. But her body, which gave birth to me, withered away in pain. There was nothing left. She couldn't go on. For the first time, I understand what is meant by the mercy of death. She found relief from pain.

One week later, I am nursing Ella in the church foyer before entering for my mother's funeral. My milk starts leaking when I give a eulogy for my mother about not being afraid to live, because death is waiting.

I receive a text from Becky. 'Hello, Sine. I just was wondering if you gave birth. Write back.'

I reply a few days later. 'My little daughter arrived on 2 June. Her name is Ella. My mother died on 11 June. So my life is joy and sorrow. I am in Denmark to bury my mother. Love, S.'

Becky writes back, 'Congratulations on the baby. I hope she is beautiful. I am so sorry about your mother. May her soul rest in peace. She's gone now. Be strong, Sine, for your baby and for yourself. Love u.'

Several days after, I'm sitting on Sommai's beige-brown sofa in her house in Thy. We drove up there after the burial in Viborg. She looks at me with compassion and asks, 'Did you make it home before she died?'

'Yes,' I say.

'That's good,' she says. 'I did not make it home for my mother's funeral.'

We have known each other now for nine years and Sommai is one of the people I feel most safe and can be most honest with. In her texts to me, she often writes, 'Hey honey, I miss you,' or 'Hey honey, I'm home tomorrow. Feel free to call.' Now she is sitting with Ella in her arms. She is one of the first people outside of our family to hold her. Ella's little shirt is green with red ladybirds. Sommai is wearing a woven Thai shirt, with her hair in a ponytail. She has just had her eyebrows tattooed. They are sharply defined in a colour between black and dark green. The cuckoo clock that Sommai got from her daughter in Switzerland is ticking. We go into the bedroom and change Ella's nappy. Over Sommai's bed hangs a black and white photo of her deceased mother in a gold frame.

I tell Sommai about a dream I had the night before. A wasp had become caught in my wavy hair. I couldn't get it out and I was afraid of getting stung on my forehead, my scalp and my fingers. Then my mother's face, but not her body, appeared in my dream. 'You have to get the wasp out yourself,' she said. 'I can't help you any more.'

Sommai nods. 'Sometimes my mother visits from Thailand,' she says. 'She sits on the windowsill over there at night and watches how things are going for me here in Denmark. She comes to watch over me.'

Sommai, the author and her daughter, Ella

Grief Therapy

Copenhagen, 2013

Eight months after my mother's death, I have my first day at the office after my maternity leave. I sit in front of the computer screen to write about the women I met in Nigeria before Ella was born, and before my mother died, and I start crying. I think that I will call my mother, but then I realise that she's dead.

I stare at my bulletin board, filled with photos from Nigeria, and I feel like I can't do it. That everything I write is terrible, that I'm a weak person, and that I have to pull myself together. I am sitting here earning a salary at the office, crying while I write about women who sell sex in Nigeria for three dollars a client. But all I can do is go to my boss and take time off. I am met with caring and understanding and I get two months' sick leave, so I can get a handle on my grief and calm down my nervous system.

My doctor, Anna, prescribes twelve sessions with a psychologist and writes the reason in my health records: 'Having a mother die and giving birth at the same time is a high-risk situation for postpartum depression.' So, I visit a grief therapist to pick up the pieces after my mother's death.

The therapist's room is white, with high ceilings and decorated with calm beige and candles. I have a choice of coffee or herbal tea. I choose coffee. The therapist drinks tea. While I talk, she writes on a paper flip chart on an easel. The marker scratches across the paper. She asks about my family and I tell her how I grew up, where and with whom. Week after week, she records the sessions and sends them to me.

She works with narrative – stories about the deceased, about ourselves, our family and our world. I don't have postpartum depression, but with the therapist, I try to understand myself, my mother and the stories in my family in new and more conscious ways. I try to connect the past with the present, to be able to envision a future without my mother.

When I listen back to the recordings, I can hear that when we dig into family stories, we focus on the women – maybe because they are connected to me and to the world I am so intent on researching.

In many ways, these sessions remind me of the way I approach stories told by the women I spend time with during my work. But in contrast to a therapist's work, my work as an anthropologist is to understand the women's stories and society's stories about them; not to introduce ideas, change or expand their stories for any therapeutic reason. They have rarely shared with anyone the worst things that happened to them. Their sex work, the children they lost, the violence they experienced, or what they saw on their journeys through Europe – it rattles around inside them, but remains outwardly unexpressed.

No one has offered them twelve therapy sessions at a discount and there's no guarantee that they would accept. Some of them have shared a bit with their mothers, with a sister or a friend, but migration often creates fleeting relationships and their families are far away. A girlfriend at a brothel might leave again after three months; the internet connection to a village in Nigeria is too poor for long, glitchy conversations about working the streets. And they are surrounded by other women who are also plagued with their own worries. They might not have the energy. To sit on a sofa and have one person listen, comfort and make connections in your life that you can't see yourself, that is a privilege.

Most of my therapy sessions quickly turn to my mother and my grandmother. We explore how their lives and stories have penetrated my family and taken root in me. On whose shoulders am I standing? Where can I find support and comfort? At the same time, it is a journey of understanding how I fit into the larger global story of feminism and colonialism, just like the women I write about.

Raised Feminist

The therapist and I talk about how to move on from grief, what it means to be the grown child of someone deceased, how to tell my daughter about her grandmother, whom she was only able to lie beside for a moment on her deathbed, and what I carry on from my mother in my life and in my work.

I tell her about Søs, my mother. From Copenhagen, a teacher, feminist and communist. She moved to the countryside in the 1970s to attend the teachers' academy and to live in a collective with my father, Viggo. On postcards, and in personal ads in *Land & Folk*, the communist newspaper, there were messages like 'Comrades, congratulations on the baby girl' and 'Sun goes up, sun goes down, we long for peace.' As a little girl, I sang the refrain to the communist workers' song, 'The Internationale': 'Arise, ye wretched of the earth'. Some of my first memories are of celebrating International Women's Day on 8 March and from the Land & Folk Festival in Fælledparken.

My mother and father were interested in communism, socialism, feminism, international solidarity, ANC's struggle in South Africa and solidarity with Chile, Nicaragua and Vietnam. My parents taught me to be on the side of revolution. My mother taught me to be on the side of women, especially.

My mother grew up in a three-room apartment in Bispebjerg, near Grundtvig's Church. My grandmother worked for a clothing manufacturer and

The mother of the author in 1973 protesting the Danish entrance into the EEC, now the EU

always voted for women. She sewed all the clothes for my mother and her five other children. My grandmother lost her own mother to tuberculosis when she was eleven, which was one of the reasons that she didn't hug much, according to my mother. She was afraid of catching something. My grandmother lost two sons, my mother's brothers, while she was alive. One had a heart attack. The other lost his job as a mason, started to drink, got divorced, then moved home to live with my grandmother. One night, he fell headfirst down a concrete stairway under her subsidised apartment while he was drunk. He didn't survive and for years after that, I was scared to look down those dark cellar stairs. Every day, my grandmother had to walk past that gaping abyss where her son fell in order to leave her apartment. She cared for my grandfather, who had Parkinson's, until he died, and in the last years of her life she refused to attend any more funerals. She had been to too many.

While talking about my mother, images of my grandmother flash before me: from a woman knitting, apple cake, *Family Journal* magazine, a knit cap over her blue-grey hair; to what she became and where my mother came from – a woman who had lost much, worked hard, raised many children and cared for others until the day she died.

After I talk for a while, the therapist will often ask, 'What feels most important in what you just told me?' And I often find that what is most important to me, what gives me strength, is when I discover fragments of my mother's life that I am able to integrate into my own, like a researcher. And in that way, she will live on.

I see more clearly now that my mother carried on

my grandmother's focus on women. My mother was especially active in the now-defunct Denmark Democratic Women's Association (DKK). They created diverse solidarity efforts with countries that were fighting colonialism, neo-colonialism and imperialism. This allowed her to combine her feminism with international solidarity. Hers was a feminism that was not interested in 'saving women in the third world', but in showing solidarity with them.

I have been critical in my work of what is called white feminism, where whiteness and Western values are viewed as superior and women's problems and struggles are made universal without taking race, class and other factors into consideration. But an abortion is not just an abortion; a birth is not just a birth; a divorce is not just a divorce; and debt is not just debt. When I look at all the stories in my notebooks, one difference between my life and theirs is that all the times my life has become difficult, I have been helped by others, by society, by therapy, by the health care system, while the women I have worked with have, by and large, had to make it on their own.

Was it my mother who led me to Thy, migrant women and sex workers? Do I see sex work as work because I grew up in a feminist, socialist household, where there was daily talk about solidarity and workers' conditions? Why am I researching what I am, in the way that I do? These are still unanswered questions. But I am beginning to understand that the type of feminism I feel akin to, I have inherited from my mother and that she inherited it from my grandmother.

Was My Grandmother a Migrant?

The therapist asks me about my paternal grandmother, Ella, whom she obviously feels I was close to. She died many years ago, while I was pregnant with Carl, shortly after my first trip to Thy. It makes sense that the therapist asks me this, because we have been talking about the love that I had received in my life from people who were deceased and how I carried with me that feeling of being loved.

In my paternal grandparents' house in Emdrup, close to the brothel where I worked briefly as receptionist, there was a zebra skin hanging on the wall and a leopard skin on the floor. There were carved ivory figurines on the shelves and paintings of black women's faces on the walls. As a child, I rested my chin on the leopard's head while I watched the Danish documentary series *Mellem Himmel og Jord* (*Between the Earth and Sky*) on television. My family had lived in South Africa and Northern Rhodesia (now Zambia) in the 1950s and as a child, I often heard stories about wild animals, sleeping sickness and the times when they lived in tents for weeks in the bush.

In our talks about my grandmother, I focus more and more on that period and I start to explore their lives there, especially my grandmother's.

My grandfather was an unemployed mason after the Second World War. He read a classified ad in the newspaper about European workers being sought for the steel mines of South Africa. He travelled there first and my grandmother followed him, with my two-year-old father and my thirteen-year-old uncle. They left with the hopes of a future with more material wealth, leaving behind unemployment and a little two-room apartment on Rådvadsvej in north-west Copenhagen. I have a photograph where my grandmother is sitting with a group of white women and children on a ship on the way to Cape Town. The women are following their husbands, which is what women did at that time.

I take out the letters that my grandmother sent home from Africa to her family in Ringkøbing, a town on the west coast of Denmark. The airmail letters are yellowed and crackle like parchment. There are red lines around the envelope edges, and on the back is written, 'If anything is enclosed this letter will be sent by ordinary mail.' The letter must only contain the words my grandmother sent home to her parents. Anything else would weigh down the plane, flying low across the African continent.

In these letters, she wrote about how the children were doing, about the new refrigerator she had installed so their food could be kept cold, about bananas in the yard, about the car they bought and about the little red house that the international mining company, Anglo American Corporation, had built, following an American design, for the white European workers in a part of the city near the mine. For my grandmother and grandfather, this was the 'American Dream', only in Northern Rhodesia: a single-family home, a yard, a car and hot water. In faded photos in a suitcase, I find my grandfather in work clothes at the smelter, where he worked as a mason seventy hours a week, building brick ovens where they melted the copper. And there is my housewife grandmother at the coffee table in the living room, with crocheted Danish daisies on the tablecloth. She looks both happy and a bit lonely in these photos.

As I read the letters, I also notice the things my grandmother didn't write about, things which I learned later were also part of her life in Africa. She didn't write about loneliness or sickness or about my grandfather's exhausting work in the heat. And she didn't write about only knowing Danish and having difficulty talking with people. And she didn't mention being admitted to a distant hospital; we never found out why.

They stayed in Africa for nine years, the two of them. They were away so long that they couldn't participate in their family life back in Denmark. One day, my grandfather received a short telegram from Denmark. It read, 'Your mother is dead.' Nothing else. Back then, every additional word was expensive and the family at home didn't have much. He wasn't able to travel home for the funeral.

When I read my grandmother's letters, it hits me how much she protected her family in Ringkøbing from the countless difficulties and dangers they encountered in Africa. In that way, she was like the migrant women I work with, who also try to protect their families. Sommai didn't tell her family how exhausting it was to have four cleaning jobs and about leaving in the early mornings on her Puch Maxi. The woman at the brothel in Thy told her family she was a cleaning assistant. Becky dreams about coming to Europe and sending home a large amount of money as a surprise, without her family knowing that she left or what she experienced on the way. They protect their families, like my grandmother did, so they won't worry.

I research migration. I see migration everywhere. I see films and exhibits about migration and sex work. I speak with other researchers about migration, but we always talk about 'their' migration. Now forgotten in the family albums are the 300,000 Danes, about a tenth of the population, who left for the USA across the Atlantic between 1850 and 1914. Most of them were men. The women followed later with the children. Other men left their wives and children to venture out in the world. The history of the migration of women is noticeably untold. And we often do not use the word 'migration' when describing white people who journeyed abroad. We call them pioneers, expats, adventurers, colonisers, missionaries and so on. White people are seldom called migrants. And I also hesitate to call my own family's travel 'migration', because today 'migration' has such raw, racial connotations and consequences. To travel abroad as a white European was not the same, and is not the same, as a black Nigerian travelling without a passport and a visa. The motivation to travel and the emotions connected to it may have many similarities, but the experiences are radically different.

My grandmother and grandfather also experienced the difference associated with skin colour when they came to Africa. My grandmother wrote a letter from South Africa to her mother and father in Ringkøbing: 'Many nights, we hear heart-wrenching screams from the police station nearby. It's the negroes who are being whipped in their cells.' This letter was one of the only mentions of anything negative and contains offensive language that we don't use today. But my grandparents became increasingly upset with the apartheid system and they left quickly for Northern Rhodesia.

In 1952, before leaving, my grandfather wrote a letter to the editor of the communist newspaper, *Land & Folk*: 'I hope that these words can serve as a warning for all Danish tradesmen who are thinking of emigrating to South Africa . . . for people who wish to be able to speak and think freely, it is a great disappointment to come to this country, which is far from democratic and free . . . if my name can be deleted, that is probably for the best . . .'

White Debt

Copenhagen, 2023

On the tall black bookshelf behind my desk, where most of this book is being written, stands a framed photo of my grandmother during her years in Africa. In the photo, she is carrying my father. He is about three. Betty, my grandmother's maid, is standing next to them. Betty is black, with short, curly hair and she is wearing a checked skirt made of coarse cloth, with pockets. One pocket is partially torn and the hem of her skirt is worn and a bit frayed. Her white collar frames her neck above her tight blue jumper. She is standing with her hands behind her back. My grandmother is white, with short, wavy hair. She is wearing a dark skirt and a matching jacket with buttons. I have her features. We both have round cheeks and you can see our teeth when we smile. They are standing bare-legged in high grass. In the background are two small white houses with metal roofs. The photo seems a bit staged, but it is obvious that the three of them are connected. Betty and my grandmother smile at the photographer, who might be my grandfather. My father is looking at Betty and he appears happy.

Once in a while, when I have had guests who are interested in race and colonialism, I have placed the photo face down. Maybe it's shame over my family's involvement, or maybe it's that I don't want them to be seen as people who took advantage of Africa and Africans. Or that my grandmother should be seen as a

The author's father as a baby, grandmother Ella and the house-maid Betty in South Africa in 1952

white woman who hired a black woman. Even though there is a story behind it, there is an asymmetry in the photo. The white woman versus the black woman.

This is about my 'white debt', a term that has recently come into focus, especially in the US, where white Americans are researching their families' connections to slavery. But it is also increasing in use among Europeans who are researching their connection to colonialism, connections which are often omitted from the family history but have been told as anecdotes and never explored more deeply. Now it is becoming more and more important for me to know about these connections. I want to know where I come from and how that plays into my research. This is not simply a genealogy project.

I call my father to ask him about that time in his childhood. He has read what I have written for my book and I want to hear his thoughts.

'I feel bad that you hide the photo of your grandmother and Betty,' he says. 'They just lie there staring into the shelf? What really happened was that Betty wanted to leave with your grandmother and grandfather, to get away from apartheid. When they left South Africa, they tried to take her with them, but she couldn't get a passport. They were sad to have to leave her behind and they gave her most of their possessions before they drove north. They kept in contact and wrote letters for many years, even after they moved back to Denmark, and your grandmother sent Betty money.

'And about "white debt",' he continues, 'you have to explain what you mean by that a bit more. I don't feel white debt. Your grandfather worked seventy hours a week in toxic fumes, which was maybe one of the reasons he died young. He was used by the huge mining companies and he protested with a letter to the editor, to warn other Danish tradespeople who could end up in a similar situation.' With indignation in his voice, he goes on, 'Those big mining companies were bloodsuckers. They're the ones getting fat on Africa's resources, not your little grandfather.'

'I can see that,' I say, wondering if I am focusing too much on colonialism, shame and blame. Questioning if he's right. Or is this a generational thing – that we look differently at what happened? He is protecting his mother and father from being misunderstood, which I also want. He was there with them in Africa; he knows what it cost them, while I am just sitting here analysing it. But he is not part of the reality of the research and the discussions I take part in every day, that I work with and am confronted by.

A few weeks later, I present parts of this book at a seminar for researchers on new ways of writing about migration. I speak about ways to write oneself into the text by looking at one's own history and I use my family's travels as an example. I have just returned from maternity leave after having my fourth child, Wilder. My brain is foggy and I am sure I do not explain what I mean as precisely as I should. One participant, a Syrian refugee, says that he thinks it is problematic for me to use the word 'migrant' about my grandmother. 'That is completely different from migrants today,' he says. I agree.

Another participant says, 'I come from Eastern Europe and I'm white, but I am triggered when you say "white". I think there are a lot of nuances of "white".' I agree.

Afterwards, white research colleagues approach me and say that there are similar stories in their family histories. But they are not about to expose their connections to a colonial past. During this period, I feel like I am in a boxing match.

I read and think about the words of the Irish-Nigerian academic and author Emma Dabiri: 'You are not responsible for what your ancestors did. You are responsible for what you do.'[xv]

My grandparents were far down in the colonial hierarchy. They did not earn a fortune, they did not have slaves and they didn't kill anyone. They had been unemployed and relatively poor in Danish terms when they left the country. But my own family history shows how far the economic consequences of colonialism reached. My grandfather earned twenty times what the black African mineworkers earned. He earned the money that made it possible for him and my grandmother to buy a modern terraced house in Emdrup, with a view of Utterslev Lake. My grandfather's work in the mine influenced our lives and lifted us into the middle class. The inheritance from my grandparents made it possible for my father and his wife to buy a terraced house north of Copenhagen. One day, I may inherit a small chunk of Africa's late-colonial potential.

Becky's Third Attempt

Copenhagen and Benin City, 2015

Becky texts me: 'I am back with my ex-boyfriend. My mother doesn't like him. He's not Muslim. But I don't care. I can decide for myself. The problem is I want to have a baby. But we have had sex lots of times and I didn't get pregnant. The doctor says there's nothing wrong with me. What should I do?'

'Have you tried using an ovulation calendar?' I answer and send a link. 'That way you know when you can get pregnant. It worked for me.'

'Thanks. If I have a baby I'll stay in Nigeria, at least for a while. If I don't have one, then I'll go to Europe.'

I write back: 'Did you hear about the 800 people who drowned on the way to Italy?' I have a naive hope that she will think twice about leaving.

'Yes,' she writes. 'I saw it on CNN. But if I get the chance, I'll go. If I die, I die. I won't stop before I make it to Italy. I am doing it for me and my family.'

A couple of months later, Becky told me that she still wasn't pregnant and that she had negotiated a price with a madam for a trip to Europe. She got it down from 40,000 euros[14] to 30,000.[15] In return, Becky has to recruit five other women to go with her to Italy. I ask her if she knows that some people will think that by finding women to go with her to Europe, she's

[14] 34,678 GBP
[15] 26,008 GBP

trafficking. 'Yes, I know,' she answers. 'But this is my chance. What if I run into problems? Do you think I should say that I'm a victim of trafficking, or that I'm running from Boko Haram?'

I answer, 'I don't know what is best to say.'

After a few weeks, Becky posts a new photo of herself on Facebook. She's in a red, low-cut body suit with a gold chain around her neck, shiny gold sandals and blue nail polish. She's looking down at her cleavage, leaning against a silver SUV.

Then she sends me a selfie of her with five women – all wearing tight dresses and blue shimmer eyeshadow. They are laughing while they drink beer from large bottles, sitting on plastic chairs at an outdoor bar in Benin City. These are the women Becky recruited. They are celebrating their departure for Europe the following morning.

On 26 July 2015, Becky leaves for Italy for the third time. I am back in Denmark after completing my PhD in New York City. I'm at work in my office in Copenhagen, following her progress on my wall map of Africa.

I put a pin in each new city she arrives in, on her way north through Nigeria. They start in Benin City. Then to Abuja, Kano, Kaduna, Katsina and over the border into Niger, to Zinder and Agadez, which she evidently reaches on 4 August. Then there are no more messages and I can't put any more pins in the map. This isn't unusual. She has changed her number countless times. She has also lost her phone to armed thieves before and often didn't have enough money to pay for the internet or was in a place without reception. I send texts for weeks.

7 August 2015: Where are you?
8 November 2015: Are you in Libya?
20 November 2015: Did you get this text?
26 December 2015: Merry Christmas. I hope you are well, and that I am not hearing from you because you are busy with other things. Love, S

My texts to her go unread.

Becky is Dead

Copenhagen, 2016

'RIP Becky. You will always be in my heart.'

This Facebook post pops up in my feed on 30 March 2016. Becky is tagged. More posts follow: 'Queen, why so soon?' 'What a world, it's like a dream when I heard you were gone . . . Rest on Becky.' 'Water run from my eyes, may your soul rest, Becky.'

My breath stops for a second. I read the posts again; my heart is pounding. It is about eight months since I heard from her last. Disbelief rises in me. Maybe it's not true. Maybe Becky wanted someone to think she was dead because she made it to Europe and she wanted to put an end to demands to repay her debt. I had heard about this before: Nigerian women 'playing dead' to get out from under debt and from their family's impossible demands for money to be sent home. But Becky had negotiated her sex work and debt herself and she left so that she could send money back to her mother and father. She wanted to impress them. She didn't leave to get away from them.

In shock, I write private messages to the people who wrote the posts: 'What happened to Becky? How did she die?' More Facebook friends also seem startled and unaware. 'Is she dead? What happened?'

A woman I don't know answers me with a private message. Becky was not in Benin City when it happened, she writes. She had left. She was up north in Nigeria, or maybe in Niger, on the way to Italy. But she got pregnant and the baby died inside her. They took her to a doctor at an old clinic, but he couldn't help. They couldn't get the baby out, so she died.

I write back to the woman. 'Do you know where she was buried? Did you go to the funeral? I am Becky's friend from Denmark and I am trying to find out what happened.' She doesn't reply.

But Becky is dead. I sit at my desk, look at the map with all the pins. The last pin is in Agadez, in Niger, just before the harsh journey across the Sahara. At some point, after that last pin in the map, after her last message to me – a big smiley face with sunglasses – she died. I don't know where and when she died, who she was with, who she was pregnant by or how far along she was.

Of all the things that could have killed Becky, it was her pregnancy that ended her life. She could have been assassinated by Boko Haram. She could have drowned in the Mediterranean. She could have been murdered by a client at a motorway rest stop in southern Europe. But she died from being pregnant. She died in a way that very likely would never have happened in Europe. Becky died because she was poor and she couldn't get help. She died in almost the same way as her friend Maria, whom she had to leave in the desert on her way back from Libya. Becky was twenty-eight years old.

I remember that we had agreed to eat ice cream together in Copenhagen in the sunshine.

Becky

Aftermath

Later, I have a brief video call with Becky's family. Her brother, wearing military trousers, and her two sisters are sitting on white plastic chairs in Becky's hometown of Michika in northern Nigeria. Her brother is holding an automatic rifle in his lap. They say they will send me photos from the funeral. But I don't get any photos and no one has yet explained to me where Becky died or where she is buried.

Becky's family fought against Boko Haram, particularly after they killed six of the family's sons. Becky wrote a text to me in 2014: 'Boko Haram bombed my grandfather's house. Six of my family members are dead. The soldiers are fighting.' Boko Haram killed Becky's six cousins in Michika, just 100 kilometres from Chibok, where, in 2014, they kidnapped 276 schoolgirls from their dormitories, the night before their final exams.

Boko Haram took the girls while they lay in their beds, studying. After graduating, they would have been some of the most educated young women in this impoverished region, where most girls never learn to read. The kidnapping received international attention. Michelle Obama tweeted #BringBackOurGirls. That was seen, liked or retweeted by hundreds of millions of people all over the world: by Hollywood stars, prime ministers, rappers; from Angelina Jolie to Oprah to the Pope. The #BringBackOurGirls campaign is one of the rare times Nigerian girls and women, like Becky, made it onto the global agenda. But, in 2023, ninety-eight girls are still being held captive by Boko Haram.

Becky's life was like a sketch of the situation in the wider world. Her life course was entwined with Islam, from which she converted; with Boko Haram, who killed members of her family; with the EU's migration control, which meant that she had to go into deep debt to travel to Italy; and with corruption in Nigeria, a rich country that does not distribute its wealth. Unemployment is widespread and the public health care system is limited, so too many Nigerian women die during childbirth as they cannot access proper medical care. One small, vibrant, dream-filled life was made difficult – impossible even – by forces beyond her control.

When I think how difficult it is for me to find out what happened to Becky, it becomes even more obvious how difficult it would be for a mother and father in Nigeria to find out what happened to their child, whom they fear may have drowned in the Mediterranean. The trail disappears. There is no one to ask. The people you thought you could reach are suddenly gone. The other women I met with Becky in Benin City know as little as I do. She didn't die there and they don't know who she was travelling with. She was her own person and she went her own way. Not being able to find out more feels like a hard shell around her death. That she could just disappear and there is no one to share the loss with me.

Becky's Facebook page remains extant. So every year on 1 October, Facebook friends who don't know she died still wish her happy birthday and she comes up in my feed. A sign that she was here. I don't write to tell them that she died.

Between Two Worlds

Thy, 2016

'I'm not sure I should stay with Niels,' says Sommai. 'I miss Thailand. I want to go back. But he doesn't want to come. He wants to stay in Denmark. He says, "Denmark is my country; Thailand is yours."'

I am finally back in Sommai's kitchen after working on my PhD in New York and doing fieldwork in Nigeria and Vesterbro. I've missed her. Niels is sitting at his computer in the living room, playing solitaire and smoking cigarettes. Sommai says, 'But I'm afraid that he will die alone if I leave him and go to Thailand.'

She and I have this conversation periodically on the phone – should she stay or go? She misses Thailand. She never meant for her bus ride to Pattaya, that day many years ago, to result in her never living in Thailand again. Working in Pattaya was a solution for her life back then. But she wants to grow old in Thailand. She wants to die in Thailand, not in Denmark. Sex work in Pattaya brought her out of poverty, but also into a marriage that carried her away from her home.

'I don't want to die in a nursing home,' she often says. That is the saddest thing she can imagine. Just sitting there, being lonely, with no family members coming to visit. This bleak image is so different from the way that the elderly are treated in Thailand, according to Sommai. People may be poor, and unable to afford hospital bills for the sick and aged, but the elders remain in their villages and continue to play a part in family life.

Their families take care of them, bring them food, give them respect. They sit together talking. This is the old age that Sommai dreams of. Her sister, Muk, still lives in Mo Baan and every time Sommai is in Thailand, her dream of growing old there takes a firmer hold.

Niels comes into the kitchen and says, 'We didn't think about that when we fell in love twenty-six years ago.' He has always been crazy about her, even though he has forgotten birthdays, bridal bouquets and other things which she asked him to remember. Even though there have been conflicts in their transnational, constructed family – especially with the children, when Sommai stood between them during teenage rebellions and unmet expectations.

But there is sorrow in Niels' eyes when he says that. As if he knows that he is not her everything, that she will always long for the country she comes from, away from him. He won't hold her back. That has always been clear between them. He says, 'She is her own person and she can do what she wants.' But he is too old to go with her. He has had two heart operations and he daren't leave the Danish health care system and the safe existence he has here. It is hard to put love into words, or to give a reason for it. The love that Niels feels for Sommai feels greater than that. And I understand. To me, Sommai is a force of nature. And it seems that she gets even stronger and more beautiful with age.

'I thought Niels would come with me,' she says. 'I mean, he would like to come and spend every winter in Pattaya and he says he can take care of himself if I go there for several months at a time. But I feel bad about him being old and sitting here all alone. He has always been there for me.'

We talk about when Sommai, after a few years in Denmark, developed the same blood illness that her sister died from, the sister whose children Sommai later supported. Several people in their village died at that time, from something the doctors from the local hospital in Isaan said was 'in their blood'. The village suspected a pesticide that young men were spraying on local fields from tanks on their backs, totally unprotected, in huge clouds that drifted over the houses and settled everywhere. They had seen the young men collapse in the fields. The Danish doctors at the hospital in Aalborg could not determine what it was, but, like the people in Mo Baan, they suspected it was pesticides.

Sommai had almost no blood inside her and dark blotches all over her body. Her sister had not survived and Sommai was so sick that Niels arranged an emergency adoption of her two youngest children, so they wouldn't be deported to Thailand if she died. The doctors tried an emergency blood transfusion on Sommai. It helped and she began to recover.

Niels' adoption of her children created a special bond between them. Sommai will never forget that he took on that responsibility. She feels this binds her to him. They are connected through the family they have created, their partnership.

I know that he also loves her for being intelligent, for giving him a new family and for sharing Thailand with him. They share a kind of defiant pride for the way they met. They never hid it from their children, but instead let the way they met be a part of their lives. I have often been out with them at bars in Pattaya. They go and talk with the women from her village who work there.

Niels says, 'I was a sex tourist, or whatever you call it,

but I was crazy about her. I was.' Some people thought that it couldn't be love when he 'found' Sommai at a bar. Niels disagrees, 'Maybe other people think they met their wife in the "correct" way – good for them. I love my wife and I am proud of all she has done for our family.' Perhaps it is a result of my own work, but to hear husbands defend their wives' sex work makes me feel hopeful and warms my heart.

Sommai also struggles with the inherent hierarchy among Thai people. In a television programme about marriage across borders, one Thai woman says that she did not meet her Danish husband 'that way' at a bar and that she is not 'one of them' – a sex worker, that is. Sommai has brought that phrase up numerous times in our conversations. '"One of them"! One of who? We are no different from anyone else.'

All that Niels and Sommai share, including their love, makes Sommai's longing for Thailand even more challenging. Sommai is full of doubt, debilitating doubt. 'I am so uncertain,' she says, 'because I want to be able to decide for myself at this point in my life. So some days, I think, I am not going to take care of any more men, no more men. I just want to do what I want, now that I am retired. I have always thought that I would return to Thailand, to my sister and my son in the village.'

Sommai's eldest son, Jenwut, stayed behind when she left for Denmark. He lives alone with his two daughters in the house that Sommai built in Mo Baan. For a few years, he tried running a grocery in town with his wife, but the circumstances were too difficult and she left him for Pattaya. She met a German man there and left with him. Now Jenwut and the two kids are supported by Sommai and his ex-wife.

Sommai and her son have a special bond, as if there is a bit of guilt and additional tenderness over not taking him with her when she left for Denmark. But he was a grown boy and it was hard to get a visa for him. Plus, she needed him to assist her ageing parents in taking care of her sister's children. So she sent them money. Sommai now has thirteen grandchildren and one great-grandchild. All the children, the grandchildren and the great-grandchild live the life they do because of her decision to leave for Pattaya.

But here in the kitchen in Thy, it feels as if all the problems she has tried to solve over the years have piled up: all her worries about the children, being split between two countries and to have followed a man abroad.

'I feel lonely here,' she says, 'but I know that I can't just go back and be at peace amid all the problems. There is no peaceful place for me anywhere.'

Somedays, she feels panicked. Imagine if she gets too old and weak to go back to live in Thailand. Imagine if she suddenly dies in Denmark and doesn't make it back. Should she give up her husband or her country?

Peace and Quiet

'I just got home from the hospital,' says Sommai on the telephone. 'I took pills, too many pills . . . It wasn't because I wanted to die, I just wanted peace. I wanted it to be peaceful around me. It was as if no one was listening to what I was saying and what I wanted. I just wanted to be left in peace.'

Hearing this is a shock. She is in Thy and I am in a taxi on the way to Bangkok airport, on my way home after working in Thailand. It is a few months since we last sat in her kitchen. The pink taxi is racing through traffic to the airport.

'Is there anyone at home with you now?' I ask calmly, although a voice inside my head is shouting, 'No! You can't do that! Never do that!'

'Yes, Niels is here, in the living room. At the hospital, they said I could speak with a psychologist in Nykøbing Mors. But I don't want to. I'm not crazy. This is about Thailand and my family. I don't know what to do, or where I belong, and everyone is always creating problems and wanting my help. I don't think a Danish psychologist will understand that.'

'Let me see if there is a Thai psychologist in Denmark you can talk to. OK?'

'I don't know,' she says. 'I don't think I need to talk to a psychologist. I think I need to figure out what I want to do, and what I have to do, now that I'm older. And I want to try to let my children live their own lives and do what they want; not worry so much about them and say no to them sometimes. Do the things I want to do.'

We talk some more. I tell her, 'I'll come over when I'm back in Denmark.'

Niels and their children are scared. When I talk to Niels, he says, 'Sommai is so depressed and it's hard, because I don't know what to do to help her.'

He and I are taking a walk down to the fjord near their house, to get out and to give Sommai some time alone. And so that Niels can have some space to talk with me. There is no wind and the water is like a perfect mirror, joining the sky with the fjord. It is as if nature has arranged this just for us. Niels looks across the water. I can see he is having a hard time keeping his emotions in check. I think again about their love and how much he has been through, has been willing to go through for her. And again, I think about all the times Sommai has had to be the strong one in her life and put her feelings aside. Maybe this is what is hitting her now. Maybe a crack has opened where she can let herself be vulnerable. She just wants a moment of peace, as she said. Just sleep. Not to have to constantly struggle.

In my notebooks, there are several notes about suicide attempts, especially among Thai women, both young and old. None of the women I have been close with have died by suicide, but many have tried. Maybe it was more a cry for help, that someone needed to do something, or stop doing something. It was an action they took because no one was listening. Sommai took pills to get peace. At a brothel in Jylland, a woman drank bleach in frustration over a relationship, debt and bad working conditions. She went to the hospital and soon afterwards was back in Thailand, working in Pattaya. Lom drank liquid fertiliser because she had had enough of being stuck between her parents and her violent boyfriend. She said they weren't listening to her.

In the weeks after Sommai's overdose, I call her regularly. She speaks softly and we talk about her family and about everything that has happened. She repeats that she doesn't wish to die, but she knows that she took enough pills to kill her. 'I don't know what it was,' she says. 'I just wanted to sleep, put my head on the pillow and sleep deeply, right away, get away from everything. It is so hard to talk with other Thais about the problems I've had with my children and that I want to go back to Thailand, and everything that has happened in my life. Everything feels like secrets, secrets, secrets inside of me. I can't tell them, because I will lose face and they will tell other people. You know how it is, Sine. In the end, I just couldn't take it any more.'

It is obvious to us both that what happened was a turning point for Sommai. That she has to let go of something she has been holding on to. But it is also as if this turning point provides her with more calm. In time, the conflict about where she belongs begins to change. She still yearns for Thailand, but she also yearns for Denmark after she has been in Mo Baan all winter. She has four grandchildren in Denmark and her children have good jobs and a life here. They take care of their houses, watch TV programmes, travel to Mallorca on vacation and have 'Say no to racism' on their football shirts when they play matches on the weekends.

Sommai starts working as a care assistant for an

older Danish man who is disabled. She also volunteers at the Blue Cross thrift shop – 'because I want to give back to Denmark' – and helps Thai women who have had trouble in Denmark. The women at the parlours know that they can always call Sommai. She drives women, whether they have insurance or not, to the hospital and to Redens Clinic in Aalborg, which provides anonymous medical care – among other services – to sex workers.

Road Trip

Thailand, 2017

The heat hits me when we step out of the plane. There is a familiar yellow tinge in the sky and the humidity feels welcoming in my lungs. I am back in Thailand doing fieldwork, together with Sommai. I asked her to come with me, this time as a paid assistant in my research project.

Sommai's eldest son, Jenwut, picks us up at the airport and we drive towards Isaan, where we have rented a room at a motel in a deserted area near a main road. It is quiet. Apart from the family that owns the motel, we are the only people here as guests. Isaan is not an area with a lot of tourists. There are only a few places to stay between the cities. While I check us in, Sommai collects fallen fruit from the car park and brings it into our room.

When we are in the village with people we know, we sleep at their homes. But for the next few weeks we will be driving around to several villages to meet women we don't know. We are taking a research road trip. Some of the women prefer to meet us and tell us their stories away from their homes. They would rather meet at a motel or hotel room, or at a restaurant.

We will also visit families where one of the women has left for Europe, or has been sent back, or is dreaming of leaving. I am trying to learn more about how debt pertains to the women's sex-work migration and how the families regard sex work and migration.

Sommai and the author at a bar in Pattaya

Tired after our trip, we sit on our beds eating the fruit that Sommai has sliced into little pieces and talk about our plans for the coming days.

Sommai gets a FaceTime call. It is Nun, whom we know from Denmark. She is alone, with the blinds drawn, at a house-turned-brothel that she rented in the woods in Jylland. She is bored, waiting for clients, so she calls us.

She is also calling because we are going to visit her family in the morning. They are going to buy a car and furniture with money Nun has sent them from Denmark. She has also sent pictures of streamlined Danish decor from Danish home magazines to Sommai's phone: Nordic white walls, grey modular sofas and black flatscreen televisions. We are supposed to show the photos to her family. She wants to make sure that Sommai can explain to her family what they should buy.

I Would Rather Have My Mother

The next morning, Sommai buys two aromatic white jasmine wreaths with red ribbons from a female street vendor. She hangs one on the rear-view mirror of our car. Most cars here have one of these wreaths as a natural air freshener. Sommai paid 20 baht each.[16] That is a lot for many people in this area, but the wreath serves not only as an air freshener; 20 baht is the price for the luck and protection that the wreaths are reputed to provide in traffic, even though they wilt and have to be changed a couple of times a week. The second wreath we save for the car that Nun's mother is about to buy today.

Nun's family is waiting for us in the car park of Big C. There are eleven of them, who sat in the back of a pickup for the trip from their village to Big C, a shopping centre with restaurants and stores for electronics and furniture. Big C is air-conditioning, shopping, a meeting place and a family trip all in one.

All eleven of them have opinions about what should be purchased, especially the two younger women. One is Nun's cousin, who is a nurse. She is the most educated in the family and her opinion counts. When the two women suggest that the speakers for the sound system they want to buy can be placed on the floor, Nun's mother says that she doesn't know about modern things. But in the photo Nun sent, the

[16] 0.5 GBP

speakers are arranged in a stereo rack. They buy a flatscreen TV, four speakers, a modular sofa, a coffee table and a brown cabinet. They also buy new locks for the doors of the house and arrange for delivery the next day.

We have to hurry now. The newly purchased car is ready and according to the monks who will bless the car, it has to be driven off the lot before eleven in the morning. Otherwise, it will bring bad luck.

We speed off to the car dealer. Nun's family drives in the pickup towards the main Toyota dealership in Isaan. It is a large, shiny, glass building with a row of pickups outside, which are in great demand in this rural area, since people, animals and crops can be transported in the bed of the truck.

When the family first began shopping for a vehicle, Nun's mother went to the Toyota dealer out in the country. Nun was frustrated because she didn't think her family had enough experience to spend this much money. She was afraid they would get cheated. 'My mother is not used to having more than $300[17] to spend at a time,' she said, 'and there are few times in her life when she did that.' But today, they will spend the equivalent of $12,000[18] in cash for the black pickup.

The keyring, with a hanging amulet, is lying in a little dish with flowers and on the front of the vehicle, a large orange flower wreath is attached to the licence plate. Sommai hangs her white jasmine wreath on the rear-view mirror.

When we work together, Sommai is my interpreter of more than language. She helps make sure necessary

[17] 224 GBP
[18] 8,967 GBP

things are done, like placing a wreath inside the car, so that people around us feel comfortable, even though we talk with them about difficult topics.

The family takes selfies with the car behind them and then makes victory signs on each side of the car with the licence plate between them. Nun ordered a plate with numbers that bring the most luck. The right number combination brings good fortune and provides protection.

I am standing in the middle of the Toyota dealership's spotless white tile floor, surrounded by TV screens with advertisements for new cars and monks who bless the cars. I think of Nun, who called us last night from Denmark from behind drawn window blinds.

She said, 'My mother doesn't understand how much I have worked, and how many clients I have had, to be able to buy them a car.' The grinning saleswoman certainly does not know that she is selling a car paid for by a woman at a brothel in the woods in Denmark. And that the payment plan she is arranging with the family – £4,100 per year for four years – means that this woman will have to keep selling sex.

I notice a bewildered young man standing and watching from a distance. He is Nun's fifteen-year-old son, Tin, who is not participating in the celebration around the truck. He is not taking any selfies.

Two monks bless the vehicle, the family applauds, and Nun's brother drives out of the gate. Sommai, Jenwut and I follow the truck back to the village. It gets parked under a carport next to the house, where the neighbours are waiting. They check out the vehicle and listen to the loud music from its stereo system, blaring out into the village. Nun's mother drinks a beer. Her hand around the bottle is rough and worn.

Tin walks into the living room and sits on the floor across from Sommai and me. He lives here with his grandmother. He has a big sore on his arm. He tells us that he fell from his scooter, racing with some of the other boys in the village.

'When your family bought the truck, everyone was so happy, but I saw you standing all alone. Why was that?' I ask him.

He hesitates, as if he's not sure if he should answer my question truthfully. He fiddles with one leg of his trousers.

'I am glad to have the things, but I would rather have my mother here.'

I look at Sommai and I can see that she is moved. We drive back to our motel.

My Body is My Plot Of Land

'It's been a long time since I've had a beer,' says Nun's mother the next day, as she rolls out reed mats for Sommai and me on the cool tiles in the living room. We are back to talk with her some more. The new furniture has not arrived yet, but the walls are freshly painted bright yellow. It is as if they are calling out for the new furniture. Nun's mother sends her niece to bring us water.

'I was really happy and proud yesterday. And to be there with all my children. That was the end to many years where everything was going badly for me. My husband was sick for several years before he died. Nun and her boyfriend got into fights and split up and I had to take care of my grandchildren by myself. I had to find things to sell so I could make money and so my grandchildren could go to school. I sold lottery tickets, grew rice, took care of silk larvae and made charcoal. A lot of people asked me how I could stand it.

'Then I tried a new strategy: to borrow money and send my children abroad to work. I had to. We owed over a million baht[19] to different private individuals. That was old debt, but now we had new debt from more loans so my children could travel and earn money.'

I recognised this strategy. Nun had explained it to me one day at her brothel. 'My family is in debt,' she

[19] 22,977 GBP

said, 'but we still own a bit of land, land we could sell and become debt-free. But it is better to keep the land than to use it to pay off debt. My body is like a plot of land that I can take with me. My body will eventually drop in value, but the land in Thailand won't.'

Nun's mother continues, 'When Nun was going to Denmark, we borrowed even more money, 350,000 baht.'[20]

'That was expensive,' says Sommai.

'It was,' says Nun's mother, 'but Nun needed plastic surgery before she left – bigger breasts and a more defined chin, so that made it more expensive. It is easier to get work, of course, if you look good. Nun got a massage job in Denmark and I figured she wasn't only giving massages. But I told her that was OK, as long as she earned money. At first she said that she wouldn't do it, become a prostitute, but that was the only option she had.'

'What do think about that?' I ask.

'I think my daughter is brave. She is taking a big risk so that we can pay our debts. The more she lives and works alone at the brothel, and has all the clients to herself, the more she earns. Nun was being chased by the police in South Korea. So when you get chased everywhere you go, you might as well be in Denmark, where the earning potential is the highest, until you get caught. Even if she does get caught and sent back, it wouldn't be a huge problem because we don't have much debt left. In two months in Denmark, she earns as much as she would in three years in South Korea. I am very proud of her. If Nun hadn't left, we wouldn't have all this, and everything would have stayed the

[20] 8,042 GBP

same. When we bought the truck yesterday with the money she sent from Denmark, that was a symbol that things worked out for us.'

I think about the debt restructuring I received through the courts after the financial crisis and my divorce left me in deep debt. I was not given any government funds, but it meant that my bank could no longer demand absurdly high interest on top of my debt. After five very financially tight years while I paid off the debt, I was debt-free. My government helped me.

Sex workers provide long-distance debt restructuring for their families.

Travel Abroad and Be Ready to Die By the Sword

'I went to the city to offer a pig head to Ya Mo,' Ming says.

Sommai and I are interviewing her. 'I hope that will get me a visa to Spain, so I can travel to Denmark,' she goes on.

It is the day before Ming is going to Bangkok for a long-awaited meeting at the Spanish embassy. She is hoping to get a tourist visa to Spain, from where she can travel to Denmark.

I have visited the statue of Ya Mo many times with women dreaming of travelling to Europe, just like Ming. They offer a pig's head, jasmine flowers, cut fruit or lighted sticks of incense. Ya Mo was a nineteenth-century Thai female warrior who is worshiped by women in Isaan and there is a large statue of her in the central square in the capital city of Khorat. There are also small statues of her in pretty much every Thai restaurant in Vesterbro. I even have one on a shelf in my apartment. Like a Thai Joan of Arc, she stands erect with sword in hand and a traditional Isaan cloth over her shoulder. She is revered for saving Thailand, and especially Isaan, from the occupation by Laos in 1826.

People say that she got the invading soldiers drunk and chased them from Thailand with her sword. Another version is that the women of Isaan were ordered to make food for the Laotian soldiers, but Ya Mo requested so many knives to prepare the food that the women were able to attack the soldiers and chase them out.

Statue of Ya Mo in Khorat, Isaan

Regardless, this is a heroine's story, about a strong woman who took charge and liberated her people with guile. Ya Mo's story resonates with Thai women. Hers is a story of leaving home, ready to die by the sword, as the Thai saying goes. These women are also ready to leave their homes and 'die by the sword' to send money back home.

While we are sitting with Ming, Sommai says, 'You know, we are very proud of her. She took her sword and fought the enemy ... When I was a little girl, if I cried over something, I was told, "You have to be strong like Ya Mo."'

In recent years, Ming has been taking care of her two children and living with her parents, while making a host of preparations to try to make it to Denmark. She had her breasts enlarged, and bought new clothes for the trip and for her meeting at the embassy. She says that she has to wear 'fine clothes, just like a businesswoman. I have to look like someone who works in a home-furnishing store who wants to have a week's vacation in Madrid.'

By visiting Ya Mo's statue, Ming hopes for divine intervention, so the coveted visa to Europe will be set into her passport. She has tried several times to leave Thailand. Whenever she drives past a temple, she says she 'folds my hands and thinks about my visa'.

Small Dreams Does Not Exist

Ming is planning to travel to Denmark with her friend Bui. So Sommai, Ming and I take the bus to Bangkok to meet her. Bui greets us in a small, hot room on the edge of the city. There are clothes, an electric kettle and a pair of flip-flops lying on the floor. She used to live in a tiny village in Isaan, but now she is newly divorced and in debt. She is renting this room in Bangkok while she works on getting her visa, just like Ming, to get them to Denmark. She went to Bangkok to be closer to 'the office', as she calls it. There is no actual office, but there is a man with a car. He is the agent whom she and Ming have paid to get them the visas.

While Bui is waiting for her visa, she works two jobs. One of them is giving massages to tourists on Chinese charter trips and the other is selling sex to Thai men at a local brothel on the outskirts of Bangkok.

'Here are all the documents a person needs to get a visa to Europe,' says Bui, handing them to me. We push the mess on the bed aside and spread out the papers in a row on the green sheet. We look at each one. There is a travel plan in English. In the margin, Bui has written notes and translations into Thai.

'The office' has planned for Bui and Ming to arrive in Spain. If they are questioned in customs, they are supposed to say that they are employed at a gift shop called Small Dreams in Bangkok and that they are in Spain as tourists. The travel plan shows that they will

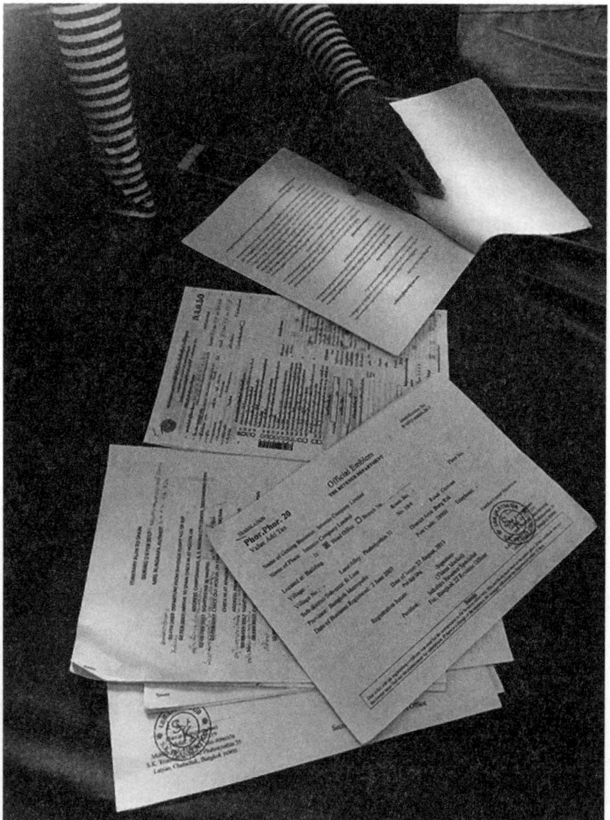

Ming and Bui's documents to travel to Europe

be in Spain for one week to see the sights in Madrid. The plan is really to spend one night in Madrid and then take a bus to Denmark.

I go with Bui and Ming into the city centre to look for the address of Small Dreams, the shop which they are going to lie about. We wander around for hours, but we can't find it. Finally, we see that the address is for a defunct shop in the exclusive expat section of town, just across from a French restaurant.

I was here a few years ago, hired by a UN project to save women from trafficking. I ate nearby with my colleagues. And now here I am in the same place with Ming and Bui.

'The office' is trying to get them visas to go to Europe using addresses and documents from the stores here, where expats and UN people eat. Bui says that, like Ming, she will wear her finest clothes, so she will look wealthy when she goes to the embassy in hopes of getting her one-week visa. 'The office' is trying to transform working women from Isaan into middle-class Thai women with connections to upscale addresses and jobs in the centre of Bangkok.

Ming and Bui don't seem very surprised that the address is made up and that Small Dreams doesn't exist. They have been preparing for months; have been operated on, have moved, have sold sex to save up and have taken out loans with high interest rates from private individuals to pay 'the office', which evidently has cheated them by giving them documents with non-existent references.

I know that by the time they seek their visas at the embassy, they will have already paid off 'the office'. I say that I'm worried the Spanish embassy will immediately find out they're lying, as soon as they google the shop, which they do in visa departments.

Ming just answers softly, 'All we can do is hope they don't google it.'

While I am writing this book, I call Sommai and read this part about Small Dreams aloud to her. I want to make sure that I understood this process the same way she did. She laughs out loud. 'Jeez, what will people think when they read it? We Thais sound stupid. That we think like that. That ambassadors don't google and that it helps to dress up in fancy clothes. Ambassadors are not idiots.'

'Should I delete the section?' I ask. 'I don't want people to think that about you.'

'No,' she says, 'keep it. It shows how good "the office" is at tricking people who don't have other options.'

Ming and Bui did not get their visas to Spain, although they did reach Denmark several years later via an Eastern European country.

The Massage Assembly Line

We go with Bui to have a look at the place where she gives massages to Chinese tourists. It is located in an industrial area on the outskirts of Bangkok. We enter a large room that resembles a gymnasium, but without the wood floor, with long tables in rows, where hundreds of Chinese tourists are eating Chinese food. All the signs are in Chinese and the restaurant is decorated with Chinese dragons and flags. While we're there, large tourist buses arrive with forty to fifty people in each one. They can try Thai massage and eat Chinese food for 300 baht.[21]

The women who work there have a small changing room where they can put on work shirts and store their handbags. A couple of women are sitting in front of mirrors putting on make-up. In front of the changing room, a small group of women is sitting eating Thai food. They are waiting for their next clients. The room is hot and stuffy, reeking of massage oil and sweat.

The place seems like a great deal for the travel company. When a person arrives out here in the heat, on the edge of Bangkok, on what looks like a construction site with two huge makeshift halls, with food in one and massage in the other, there is nothing else to do. At home, they might have imagined a beautiful Thai massage parlour with incense, plants, a wooden

[21] 7 GBP

The massage assembly line on the outskirts of Bangkok

interior and an authentic wellness atmosphere. But instead, there are fifty mattresses with brown plastic covers laid out in rows and dingy curtains that create the only barrier between them, resembling a continuous dormitory on a cement floor. It looks like a massage assembly line.

Bui explains to us, 'Besides the 100 baht we receive from the travel agency, we can earn more if the men say yes to "extra service" under the towel. We get that money too. So we try to sell that too, so they'll want a "happy ending". For some Chinese people, being a tourist is totally unfamiliar and they don't know what we mean when we say "extra service". So then we have to grab "that" and say 100 baht, so they understand what we mean. A lot of them say yes, even if their wife is lying on the mattress next to them behind the curtain. They bought a package trip to see temples and markets. Sometimes it's their first time abroad, so everything is pre-arranged. But often they smell really bad, because they've been driving around in the bus all day, so I don't always offer "extra service".' Her colleague nods; she has evidently had a similar experience.

The Display

After visiting the massage assembly line, Sommai and I drive to a brothel where a woman is working while she waits to go to Denmark. It is located on a noisy bypass, but behind the closed doors it is quiet. It always feels awkward to visit brothels during the day; not because of the women I meet with – they know why I'm there – but because the bartenders and cleaners have a chance to get a good look at me. The music is not playing, as it would be in the evening.

This brothel employs older women who are looking for short- or long-term work, to earn money to pay for some economic commitment. The clients are older Thai and Chinese men, not tourists, but locals. At night, it gets very busy and the red benches where the women sit behind a pane of glass, as if on display, are completely full, so men can look at them and point out which woman they wish to accompany to a room on the second floor. But right now, there are only five women working. The glass-enclosed area is nearly empty. A gnarled, older man comes in at the same time as us. One of the women gets up from her red seat and emerges through a glass door, and they go up the stairs together.

I have to use the toilet, so I follow the man and woman past the women behind the glass. They all look to be over forty and they look like women who have worked hard and have had several children. Upstairs, there are holes in the worn, dark green rug and there are seven or eight wooden doors into what must be rather small rooms, just room enough for a bed. Three of the doors are closed, as women are inside with their clients. I have never been to a brothel this shabby before. The bathroom floor is wet from a leaky sink. It seems as if nothing works. The soap dispenser is empty and there are no towels. The dustbin is full. All the people here look like they are about to fall asleep.

Sommai has located Dai, whom we are supposed to speak to. She comes out and sits with us at one of the black painted tables. We drink soft drinks.

Dai is from a village near Mo Baan and she wants to go to Denmark. She has met a Danish man, Hans, who was recently in Thailand to visit her at her village. But Dai is frustrated, because he doesn't understand why he has to pay for her trip to Denmark. He thinks she is trying to trick him. He's not convinced that they will end up staying together. Also, Hans doesn't understand why he has to send her money while she is waiting for her visa for Denmark, because his money will be wasted if they don't become a couple. He wants to know that he is getting his money's worth, as they say. He is afraid that Dai is asking for money because she is not serious about him, while Dai thinks that if he doesn't send money, then he must not be truly interested.

Sommai shrugs. She tried to talk to Hans a few days ago. 'I tried to explain to him,' she says, 'that it's better if he sends money to you until you get your visa. But he is very Danish in this way, very suspicious. I don't want to waste any more time trying to convince him. If he wants to have a Thai girlfriend, then he's going to have to understand some things. Try to see it from your side. You can't stay in your village with no money and pay for your ticket to Denmark. You have expenses at your house in the village and two children. Last time he was here, you said that he just wanted to have sex all the time, but that he wouldn't pay for your food. That is not going to work.'

Sommai says she thinks that he is serious. 'It's just that he doesn't understand what it means for you when he says no. That it means you have to work here.'

'No, I can't tell him about my job. Then he won't want me. He's jealous already.'

Dai has to return to the display behind the glass. Maybe she can land some of the afternoon clients.

Ping Pong

Copenhagen, 2015

'Come on, darling, come sit with me,' Sommai says in an alluring voice, patting the bed. 'What do you want me to do?'

It is 2015, and Sommai is portraying a sex worker in an immersive play we are attending in Vesterbro. Ping Pong, an experienced sex worker visiting from Thailand, is acting out an interactive, intimate scene in a room with bed and bathroom, decorated like a Thai hotel, which acts as the stage. Through her more than twenty years as a sex worker, she has had Thai and Western men as clients, friends, lovers and acquaintances. Ping Pong portrays her life as sex worker, with the audience as her clients.

I have invited Sommai and Niels to see this play with me, and we are three of the ten audience members who can fit into the hotel room. Ping Pong invites one 'client' up at a time, directed by her to play out a little scene which recreates some of the meetings she has had with clients. Ping Pong plays herself and we sit on chairs around the bed, representing different kinds of clients: an old and less virile one, a young backpacker with a guitar, a family man; one who is shy, one who is in love, one who is violent.[xvi]

When Ping Pong invites Sommai up, she reverses the roles. 'Now I am the client,' she says, 'and you are the sex worker.' The present sex worker and the former sex worker sit together on the bed. Sommai takes on the role.

While the rest of us 'clients' bumble about, awkward and stiff, Sommai looks professional, as if she is in touch with the work she did many years ago. Niels sits on his chair nodding, as if to say, 'Yes, that's how it is. That's the way it was, like that.' Niels remembers what it was like as a client.

Ping Pong is only in Denmark with her show for a short while, but she has been active for many years with the Thai organisation EMPOWER. The group fights for sex workers' rights and I feel solidarity with their work and their perspective.

After the theatre piece, Sommai and I enjoy colourful drinks at the Thai Corner cellar bar on Istedgade, with Ping Pong, several women from EMPOWER and the ladyboys who work at Thai Corner. Ping Pong and Sommai converse uninterrupted. Sommai listens, then starts talking energetically. She has never spoken before with anyone who works as a political activist for sex workers.

Ping Pong will not be in Copenhagen very long, but Sommai and I will visit her on our road trip in Thailand.

Thailand's Honour is Not Found in a Pussy

Thailand, 2017

Ping Pong is currently living in Khorat and Sommai and I drive out to visit her one afternoon. We haven't seen her since that evening at Thai Corner. Sommai and Ping Pong greet each other warmly.

'I am helping my mother for a few months,' Ping Pong says, as she points around the little dress shop where her mother is sitting in an office chair behind the counter. Lacy dresses hang all around us. 'Soon I will go back home and continue my work,' she says. 'But right now I am needed here.'

'Are you still working with EMPOWER?' asks Sommai. 'I've been thinking about your work since we met in Denmark. What you are doing is so important. It helps everyone who has worked at a bar to know that we are not alone. I didn't know that anyone who thought like you even existed.'

'I am still working there. Right now, we are fighting against the numerous police brothel raids in Thailand. Once in a while, the politicians decide that Pattaya needs to be cleaned up, to show that Thailand is doing something about sex work. But they do it mainly for the sake of the tourists.'

Sommai nods. 'Right, because they think we are embarrassing our country.'

'I know,' says Ping Pong. 'They say they are doing it to preserve the honour of Thailand. But the raids don't help the sex workers. They just take away their jobs.'

'Thailand's honour is not found in a pussy,' snickers Sommai, rolling her eyes. The two women laugh.

Ping Pong provides us with contacts at sex worker organisations in Pattaya and we visit them over the following weeks.

At our meetings with the Pattaya activists, who test sex workers for HIV, distribute condoms, and offer screenings for STDs and pregnancy, I note again Sommai's enthusiasm and interest. She speaks to everyone we meet and listens to their struggle against criminalisation, stigmatisation and violence against sex workers from the police, institutions, clients, lovers and partners. After these meetings, my conversations with Sommai also become more political.

Mary Jane and BMW

Mo Baan, 2017

After the visit with Ping Pong and the sex worker organisations in Pattaya, I return alone to the village to spend my last days in Thailand with Lom and her two children – Mary Jane, named after Spider-Man's girlfriend, and BMW, named after the car. She calls them MJ and BM. Lom gets a certain, very special, loving look in her eyes when she gives them baths, lies on the bed with them taking selfies or even when she just talks about her 'babies', as she calls them. I have never seen her give that look to anyone else.

Since she had MJ, Lom has not worked in Pattaya, but has been living with her parents in Mo Baan. MJ's father has left and Lom does not know where he is. BM's father is from a village nearby and she had hoped for a family life with him: mother, father and two children. He got a job at the factory on the main road. The new Chinese owners there have strict rules and the pay is low, but it's the only job available.

The last time I was here, I saw him leave every morning for work on his scooter. But in the evenings, he went out, used his pay on Thai whisky and came home late. He and Lom fought and he started to hit her. Her father and mother were displeased with their son-in-law and Lom was miserable, stuck between her two little kids, her parents and an oppressive boyfriend. When she found out that he had cheated on her, they had big fights and that was when she attempted suicide with fertiliser. After countless attempts to make up and new outbursts, she gave up on her dream of a family with him.

'I became a single mum,' she says. 'Single mum' – that is how she often describes herself when she talks about her life and explains the choices she made. But it is also a term she has started using on Facebook, when she makes flirty posts to try to attract men: 'Single mum looking for company,' she writes over a filtered photo, where the wrinkles and imperfections on her skin are smoothed out and her eyes appear larger than they are in real life.

When Lom works the village cornfields, she wears green trousers and a large, wide-brimmed, green felt hat with pink ribbons. We drive out to the fields and she shows me where she waters the corn. She can tell by feeling the leaves that some of the plants are about ready to harvest. It gets dark while we are out there and she turns on her scooter lights so we can see.

I ask, 'Do you come out here alone in the dark?' I notice that I feel a bit anxious being out in the dark among the tall cornstalks in the mud.

'No, that scares me. It's just because there are two of us here,' she says. 'I didn't used to be afraid,' she goes on. 'But recently I was knocked down between the plants by a man from the village. I know him. He was drunk. But people here know what I did for work before I had children. The men think they can just have sex with me. That night I kicked him away. He yelled that I was just a hooker and that I want it. He wasn't able to rape me. But now I only come out here alone when it's light out.'

Lom with her children and the author's daughter, Ella, in Mo Baan

Nurse

Every day, Lom's mother, Samarn, sits sunken in her wheelchair in the shade of the courtyard. Ten years ago, I sat with her on the blue sofa and she showed me around the house, telling me about when she went to Pattaya with Sommai, but turned back and married Lom's father. Back then, she dreamed that Lom would find a foreign husband. But they are both back in the village now and Samarn is terminally ill with kidney disease.

Lom takes care of her, washes her, feeds her, changes her adult nappy. They can't afford dialysis at the hospital, so for several years Lom has been giving her dialysis daily at home. She removes the plastic bags with the yellow liquid and puts them behind the house, where they lie in a pile in the sun, until there are too many and they are hauled away. While I am there, we drive to the hospital with Samarn several times. Once she is picked up by an ambulance, because they couldn't get her into their car.

Today, Lom's father is frying fish for his wife on the gas burner outside, but Samarn can hardly eat any of it. Her skin gets itchy in the heat. Lom tries to scratch her back, but her skin is so thin that it hurts. Lom sits next to me beneath the shade of the roof's overhang. She looks tired. She has been up since five o'clock this morning, helping her mother, then getting her children off to school and then working in the fields.

'I have been allowed to stay home for a while without

my father saying that I have to leave and make money,' says Lom, 'because I'm the only one who will care for my mother ... Last time, before my sister went back to England, we had a meeting – my father, her and me. It was also a bit of an argument. My sister did not want to take care of our mother and she also makes more money than me. Even though I help in the corn-fields, my father always says that I have to leave and find work as soon as my mother dies. He has always thought of me as the problem daughter. I can never make him happy. All he can see is what my sister is doing in England. My father and my sister say that I have to think of my children, that I have to leave to be able to support them. But I think BM is still so little. My father says he will take care of them as long as I leave to find work.' Lom stands up to get some water for her mother.

A couple of days later, Sommai returns from Bangkok to visit her old friend Samarn. It feels like a last good-bye. Samarn and Sommai are the same age – fifty-six. Samarn is sitting in her wheelchair in the courtyard, fanning flies away from her sores. Sommai is wearing a newly ironed blue shirt and her red-streaked hair is tied back in a ponytail. Her skin is bright and smooth and she looks so healthy next to Samarn, who is bloated, her voice weak.

Sommai sits down and takes Samarn's hand. The two old friends sit there quietly. Sommai whispers something.

I am sitting nearby with Lom, following along, but also giving them space. I cannot help but think about that bus trip they took together to Pattaya. The difference it made in their lives. Sommai stayed and met

Niels, while Samarn returned to her boyfriend, Lom's father. Sommai was also severely ill in Denmark, but was treated at the hospital in Aalborg. Samarn went back to her village and kept living her life, with demanding work in the fields. She would be able to survive her illness if she was in Denmark. But Sarman stayed in the village – the village that Sommai misses so terribly.

Mum's Hand

'Mum's hand, Mum's hand,' sobs Lom, as Samarn's coffin moves into the crematorium oven. She takes hold of her dead mother's hand in the open casket, among the fresh flowers and cigarettes that guests have laid inside to send her on her way. When the coffin is pushed on the rails into the oven, she has to let go.

The flames surround Samarn's coffin and the steel door smacks shut, locking it inside the inferno. Smoke snakes out of the crematorium's high chimney and spreads above the temple courtyard. There is a series of loud bangs, like fireworks, then it is quiet again.

A framed portrait of Samarn as a young woman, along with strings of lights, artificial flowers and incense, stood by her coffin in front of Lom's house for three days. There were flower wreaths on the ground from family, neighbours and friends. Monks sat on a little stage leading rituals for several days, to ensure Samarn a good transition to her next life. It should be a comfortable trip with flowers and cigarettes, which are needed for the journey. People arrived with food, clothes and money for the monks and hoped for their own good karma in return. Lom's older sister arrived from England. She carried the portrait on the way to the crematorium, while Lom walked behind her crying.

It takes about five hours for Samarn's cremation. Afterwards, Lom gathers the ashes into an urn. She also selects some pieces of bone to save. She brings the bone fragments and the portrait back to the house.

A few days after the funeral, Lom and I return to the temple and sit at a little fire the monks have made with leaves and branches they gathered from the grounds. In the middle of the day, it is totally quiet here, while people are out working in the fields and the children are in school. There is just Lom, me and the ashes of the dead, which are encased in the masonry walls around us. 'I have to decide soon what I want to do,' says Lom. 'There's not enough money in Pattaya right now to make it worth going there. There are only poor tourists coming in. Chinese, Russians and Muslim men. They don't spend much. They buy beer and sit out in front of the bar instead of going inside so we can make some money. They only want "short time" with the women and they always haggle over the price. I need to find a place where I can earn more money.'

I know Lom is right, because several female bar owners in Pattaya have told me how the clients back when Sommai was in Pattaya, up to when Lom left Pattaya, were mostly from Europe. They came for two or three weeks on their holidays from work, and they came for sex and relaxation. But now more men are in Thailand on business or sales trips. They work for cheap hotel chains or are attending conferences with new products to sell in Asia. These newer tourists come from Russia, the Middle East, South Korea and China. Then there are Russian families on package vacations, and families from the Middle East.

Lom says, 'I've heard about some women from my

old school who went to Malaysia. The airline tickets are reasonable and I could get a job at a massage parlour where my old classmates work.'

'But how do you feel about selling sex again?' I ask. Lom is now thirty-four. It is five years since she left Pattaya. She has had two children, worked in the fields and taken care of her sick mother. Back then, Lom always had her make-up handy, was constantly putting on more lip gloss or mascara. Now, her skin is no longer smooth, for which she blames pollen and the pesticides from the tall cornstalks that brush her face when she walks through to water them every day. Her toenails are short and flaked with fungus and dirt from walking barefoot or in thin socks in the muddy fields. She says that after her pregnancies, she has gained fifteen kilos. She used to straighten her hair and get extensions, but now she lets it become curly and frizzy. She wears hoop earrings and says that the men she meets online think she's African. 'Then being big doesn't matter so much,' she says.

'I was in Pattaya a few years ago,' she says, 'with a girlfriend who works there. I had my children with me and there were young women sitting at the bar. Thinking about these women makes me realise I couldn't work there now. The others would gossip about me, and I would never get taken by a client. I would just think I was ugly. I would be embarrassed about sitting there, comparing myself to the other women. I have to find a place where they also want older, bigger women like me. They say Malaysia has that, but there is also a woman from another village who went to Dubai. She earned a ton of money and she is also older, like me. She is thirty-nine and she hasn't been in Pattaya.

Lom's life in her village with her two children after selling sex in Pattaya

I know the work and I know what you do to earn the most money. I just have to get back into it.'

A few months after the funeral, when I'm back in Denmark, Lom sends me a video of her from a barstool in Pattaya. She has straightened hair, made-up eyes, shiny lip-glossed lips and is wearing a tight red T-shirt. She's working. 'So here I am,' she says, while filming the bar so I can see it. There is music thumping in the red lights and clients and women are sitting at the bar. She points the camera at her face and keeps talking. 'It's OK here. There's work. Not a lot, but my father is watching my kids and I can send him money. He isn't mad about my not working any more. But I'm still thinking about going to Dubai.'

Vivian

Sicily, 2017

'Hop in, we're heading to Stella Maris. You can meet Vivian.' Sylvia waves me into the front seat of her car. I slam the door and she speeds away. We leave Catania behind us and race south along the east coast of Sicily towards Syracuse. Sylvia is a Sicilian social worker and when I tell her about my work, she says she would like to help me.

This is my first time doing fieldwork in Sicily. I am staying in an apartment in the centre of Catania, the largest city on Sicily's east coast, with a view of the Mediterranean and the harbour where Doctors Without Borders has docked rescue boats, from which they disembark migrants they have saved from drowning in the sea. From my balcony, I see a long row of white tents along the wharf ready to receive the migrants. I have three children with me: the two big brothers, Julius and Carl, will be watching their little sister, Ella.

Stella Maris, a women's centre, is located in a quiet, run-down residential area. It's on the second floor and if you didn't know there was a centre for women who had crossed the sea inside, you wouldn't notice it. There is a baby gate at the top of the stairs and Disney posters line the walls. Sylvia says, 'That's new, because a child fell down the stairs last week. The child is fine, but there are a lot of children living here.'

Inside the centre, I am introduced to the director.

We sit at her desk and I explain why I came. 'We are seeing more and more Nigerian women come to Denmark to sell sex and many of them have crossed the Mediterranean to Sicily.'

The director nods despairingly. 'Yes, we are receiving a lot of women now. We are completely full and we have no place else to send them.'

She leads me out and opens doors to several rooms where the red curtains are still drawn. It is eleven in the morning and the women are lying under thick, warm blankets in single and bunk beds, some with the blankets pulled over their heads. 'They're still sleeping,' says the director. She leads me on. All the rooms are fully occupied. I think about the empty rooms at the centre in Benin City. A few women are waking up. They poke out their heads, warm and sleep-drunk, wearing earphones. It is as if they are lying in their own little worlds without sound or light under the blankets.

The director continues, 'They're unemployed and there's nothing for them to do. They go out at night into town and come back late. This isn't a prison, so they can do whatever they want. Some of them don't come back. Maybe those are the ones you meet later on in Copenhagen. There is no work for them here in Sicily, so they leave if they can. They can't leave Italy if they have applied for asylum, but they have families in Nigeria that are expecting money and they have debts to pay, so they can't just wait for their documents to go through, if they ever do. Most of the ones from Nigeria are not granted asylum.'

I don't want to see any more rooms. It feels too invasive to enter their rooms while they're sleeping. I tell the director, 'Just let them sleep.'

'You have to meet Vivian,' she says. This is the woman that Sylvia also wanted me to meet. She opens the door to a room where a woman says, 'Welcome' right away. The curtains are open and light from the sun is streaming in. A little child is sleeping in a single bed. There is a crib next to it, but the baby is in his mother's bed. 'I'm Vivian,' she says. 'This is my son, Kindys.' She points at the baby and at the bed. 'Do you want to sit down?' she asks. The director says she has something to take care of, so Vivian and I can sit and chat. The director closes the door on her way out. There aren't any chairs, so I sit on the extreme edge of the bed so as not to wake Kindys.

'How old is your son?' I ask softly, in English.

'Two years old,' she says, also in English. 'You speak English?' she asks.

'Yes, I'm not Italian. I'm from Denmark.'

'That's good,' she says, 'I'm not Italian either. So we can talk together. Most of the white people here don't speak English, so they don't understand me.' I look at the wardrobe behind her. On it hangs a photo of a woman in hospital scrubs, holding up a newborn. Vivian follows my gaze. 'My baby was born just as I arrived in Italy. That was the day he arrived, into the arms of an Italian nurse.'

I tell her that I have three children at the moment, waiting for me in Catania. 'I have three children too,' she says happily, in the voice people use when they find they have something in common with a new acquaintance. 'I have two older boys in Nigeria, but they didn't come with me to Europe. They live with my sister. I haven't seen them now for four years and they've never met their new little brother.'

'Where do your sons live in Nigeria?' I ask, already pretty certain I know what she will answer.

'They live in Benin City, where I'm from,' she says.

'I've been there several times,' I say.

She brightens up. 'You've been there? I've never met anyone here in Italy who has been to Benin City.'

We both speak English, we aren't Italian, we both have three children and we both know Benin City. That's enough for now – a start. We chat a bit more about Benin City, about Nigeria and Italian food. Vivian is tired of pasta.

Then I say, 'I'd better get back to the others.' I don't want to impose on her any more. She asks if I'm on Facebook and we become Facebook friends. 'Can I write to you?' I ask. 'Yes, please do,' she says. 'See you later,' I say, closing the door behind me.

A Real Home

A few days later, Vivian and I meet at the harbour. Kindys is in a pushchair. I buy us coffee and a little ice cream for him. Suddenly, it feels overwhelming to be sitting with Vivian, drinking coffee and eating ice cream with a child, when that was what Becky and I had talked about doing if she made it to Europe and we met in Copenhagen. Vivian is sitting here in Sicily and Becky is buried somewhere in Nigeria. Just imagine if Becky could have sat here with us. Vivian and Becky are not dissimilar. Becky was more raw and edgy, while Vivian is more open and chatty, but both of them were determined to change their lives, to get as much as possible out of their circumstances.

I tell Vivian that I knew someone named Becky from Benin City and that she died on her third attempt to make it to Europe. 'A person must never try a third time,' she says flatly. 'It always goes wrong.'

I want to defend Becky's third attempt. There were so many reasons behind her choice. But she did die on her third try and Vivian has seen a lot more friends and acquaintances cross the desert and the ocean than I have.

We talk a bit about the current situation in Benin City. 'There are a lot of kidnappings,' she says. 'They even kidnap people of moderate means. This is the way some young men earn a living. There are no jobs for them.'

It is not easy to get the opportunity to meet and talk

Vivian walking around her new neighbourhood in Sicily

to women who live at a centre, or a 'camp', as they call it. They don't have another place to live, and they often share rooms at the centre. Vivian says she has nothing to hide, so we could meet in the common area, but in the following weeks we usually meet outside – on a stairway, on the way to the supermarket or at a cafe where we drink cola in the unmerciful Sicilian heat. Vivian is constantly worried if I am too hot or too cold. She always wants to make sure I'm comfortable.

Vivian is not permitted to have overnight guests, but she suggests smuggling me into Stella Maris because she wants me to sleep over. 'You can just sneak out before the sun comes up,' she says. 'Someday I will invite you over to my own house, just like normal girlfriends.'

Sometimes, she and I end up in unforeseen situations when we are looking for a place to meet up. The Sicilian buses don't always come, and on one occasion we wander in the heat down a long side street without pavements as cars speed past. We look for water, but all the shops are closed. We didn't realise it was a holiday and we can't find any toilets, so we have to pee behind a tree along the road.

Sometimes, I ask if we should take a taxi when we go out, as the heat is so deadly. I offer to pay for a taxi to a meeting with her lawyer, to make life a little easier for her while I'm around. But Vivian considers it a waste of money. She makes a face and obviously thinks that I am not careful with my money. She says, 'You can spend your money on something else. We can walk, just like we do in Nigeria.' I remember my fieldwork with Vivian in Sicily as long walks along hot roads, dark alleys in ramshackle public housing complexes, a full bladder, Kindys tired in our arms, and laughter.

Eighth Month

The day that Vivian tells me her real reason for leaving Nigeria, we are sitting on some steps on a damp Sicilian afternoon. We don't have anywhere else to go. We are in the shade of a balcony by a building near Stella Maris. She has brought food – Nigerian chicken in spinach with lots of hot peppers. We went food shopping at Lidl the day before, hoping we could eat together. We have two hours before she has to get back to the centre. Someone is watching Kindys for her.

I had written down in my journal that Vivian had several abortions before leaving for Italy. I added a question mark after it, because I didn't ask more about them or why she mentioned them the first time we talked about why she left Nigeria. Today, we agree to talk about that some more. I say, 'You told me before that you left because you were poor, but sometimes you've also mentioned other reasons for leaving, like because your husband treated you badly. You also mentioned abortions or an abortion. Will you tell me more about that?'

While she answers, she divides up the rice and the spinach dish into two bowls. 'My husband and I had two sons; when I left they were two and three years old. When we met, he was sweet, different than many men. He washed dishes, did laundry. I could tell that he was always thinking of me and wanted to take care of me. But after we had the two boys, things changed. He only had various short-term jobs and life was hard.

He started to hit me and to drink. He often stayed out and we fought all the time.

'I got pregnant again with our third child while I was still nursing our second, who hadn't turned one yet. I always tried to plan out between my periods when we shouldn't have sex. You know, right in the middle. But since I had recently given birth and was still nursing, my period hadn't come, so I didn't know when it was safe. My husband wouldn't use a condom and didn't want to wait until I was ready and had my cycle under control again.

'I really didn't want to have another child then; maybe I didn't want to have any more at all. But he said I should keep it, that I couldn't have an abortion and his parents didn't want me to have one either. As my belly grew and the baby started kicking, I decided I wanted to have the baby after all. But when I was in my eighth month and my belly was huge, suddenly he didn't want the baby any more. He said I had to get rid of it or he would leave me. I wouldn't do that; the baby was ready, kicking every day. I refused.

'He took me to a doctor, who also refused to do it. There was a human being inside me. But then my husband found another doctor, or a man – he might not have been a doctor – a kind of pharmacist. I don't know exactly, but he said he would kill my baby for 100,000 naira.[22] I don't know where my husband got the money; he must have borrowed it. The "doctor" gave me a shot in my behind, some pills that I had to insert up inside myself and something I had to drink. Then my husband drove me back home.'

I am sitting there on the steps in the rain, trying

[22] 51 GBP

to take in all that she's telling me. I can tell that she wants to talk about it. This is more detailed than the times we have talked before, and doesn't need my careful prompting. In spite of this, I ask, 'Couldn't you do anything to stop it?'

'No. In Nigeria, the man is in charge. I couldn't stop it, but deep inside, I thought that I would never forgive him for killing an innocent baby. But it never really made a difference, because he lost interest in me after this and I guess I got used to that. I felt so ashamed that I was not able to protect my own child.

'That night, blood started gushing out between my legs.' She points at a large, brown plastic planter in front of us. 'I probably could have filled up two of those . . . My husband wasn't there. I don't know where he was. I was alone. Clumps came out – that was the baby, but it was in pieces, and shrunken, as if there was nothing under its skin. I flushed it all down the toilet.

'I kept bleeding. It hurt so bad, I don't know how to describe it. I couldn't hold it in. Our neighbour heard me yelling and she took me to the hospital. The placenta was still inside me. The doctor at the hospital removed it. They said that what I had done was illegal. They could see that I had been very pregnant and that the baby was gone. I told them my husband had done it and they said I should tell the police. If I had the strength, I would have turned him in, but I didn't. I thought that God would punish him, that Ayelala, the spirits, would punish him. I could forget that he hit me, but I can never forget that he killed our baby and didn't care about me. So I left him.

'Later, I found out that he had another woman and that she was pregnant at the same time I was.

He didn't want to have two children with two different women at the same time. He wanted to be with her and for that he would kill our baby. But her baby died too. That is, it didn't survive. But I know that was God's punishment for killing our baby; that's why the other one died too.

'He still calls me here in Italy. He wants me to forgive him. We talk about our two kids. He asks me to send him money, but I won't. I am not his bank account. He just drinks it up. He hasn't changed.

'But yes, I left because he killed my baby. He hit me and I couldn't be with him any more. I had to get away. I didn't want him to control me any more, because everything he decided was always wrong and I was right in the end.'

'What do you mean,' I ask, 'by "everything he decided was wrong"? Can you give me an example?'

'Let me see,' she says, 'an example . . . It's more of a general problem, the way men think, you know?' She explains, 'I have a schoolbook and I have to do homework. I'm not sure if what I did was right, so I ask him. I would like us to talk. He says that he knows the answer and he's feeling proud of himself. He tells me the answer. "Write this," he says. I say that I don't think that's right. He says, "But you don't know what you're talking about. Just write what I said." So I go to school and show it to the teacher. The teacher says it's wrong. I go back home and tell my husband that what he said was wrong, according to the teacher. My husband says "How do you know the teacher is right? You don't know anything." He is impossible to argue with, because it's stupid from the start. Do you know what I mean?' She gives me a helpless look.

'Yes,' I say, 'I know what you mean.'

We sit in silence. 'When I tell you all this,' she says, 'I feel all furious again.' She stares straight ahead. 'I left because I wanted to get away from everything that reminded me of him. But I also had to take care of our two boys, because he didn't. I was poor, but I left because of the dead baby and to be able to send money home to the two children I had already. My husband was no help.

'My husband stayed away for a long time after that. Maybe he was with the other woman, maybe he was afraid that I would turn him in. I started to see an old friend from school who had always wanted to be my boyfriend. He had been away for many years in Hausaland, in northern Nigeria, and when he came back, I had two children already.' She laughs. 'He should have stayed in Benin City. Now he was more like a friend and he was glad to help me to go to Europe. One of his cousins, Tony, was looking for girls to travel overland to Libya. That's through the desert, because an airline ticket is too expensive. I asked if I could be sure of not being cheated. He said, "Yes, but you know the work that the girls do in Libya. Prostitution." I said, "OK, I'm ready." My father didn't own any land and I had nothing I could sell.

'My ex-husband came by with 1,000 naira[23] for me to buy food for the kids. He tried a few times to give a bit of money, I think because he hoped I would forgive him. But I used the money on a bus ticket for me and my children, so I could take them to my mother.'

I think of Sommai's story, about when she left for Pattaya. One of a woman's duties before she leaves is to take her children to someone she can trust. Both

[23] 0.5 GBP

Vivian and Sommai remembered, years later, the price of the bus and how they got the money for it.

'We got there late,' she continues. 'My mother came out of the house and asked, "Why are you coming here at this hour?"

'"I'm leaving at sunrise," I said. "I'm here to leave my children with you." I've never been close with my mother, so she was surprised. But my father was too poor to leave them with him. My mother and father are divorced.

'I put my kids to bed and gave them one last hug. They were very little and didn't really understand what was happening. I felt terrible. The next morning, I met up with the other girls at the bus and headed to Abuja. That was the first stop on the way to Libya. My mother said that my children cried for weeks and were looking for me. But then they got used to my not being there. I haven't seen them since. I think about them every day and I feel like I can't really rest until I see them again.'

We talk about personal topics a lot, but this – sitting on a step in the rain, eating Vivian's Nigerian food and hearing her talk about the two kids she had to leave behind, and about her dead baby – is more personal than before. 'Thank you for sharing all of that with me,' I say, at a loss for words. 'You have been through a lot for your children, and you have lost a lot.'

'Now we're not just friends,' she says, 'but sisters. I have never sat with a white woman like this before, in the rain, talking about my life.'

The Brothel in Tajoura

Vivian knew that she was going to be a sex worker in Libya. Sex was what she had to sell to finance her trip from Nigeria. Sex work was a means to an end – reaching Europe. She made a deal with her old friend's cousin, Tony, that she would pay him 550,000 naira[24] for the journey to Libya by selling sex there. When she had paid it off, she would be free to keep going and cross the sea to Italy. 'I trafficked myself to Libya,' she said, 'but my trip to Italy was not trafficking.'

Vivian left, just like Becky, to drive through the Sahara Desert in the back of a pickup truck. She was with other women that Tony had made deals with. The trip was rather easy, in contrast to Becky's. Tony wanted to be sure to receive the money coming to him, so the women had to arrive safe and ready to work. He wouldn't earn anything on dead women. That's why he provided a truck that wouldn't break down, hired smugglers who knew the route well and paid bribes so they could cross the borders and checkpoints with 'his goods'.

Vivian and the other women were installed in an apartment in a one-storey building, on a quiet street in a little coastal town on the Mediterranean. A Nigerian couple managed a discreet brothel there, and ensured everything went smoothly. They only had a few women in the house, who were not allowed to leave for fear of

[24] 280 GBP

being discovered. The clients came and went quietly. In this way, they could avoid attracting the attention of the Libyan police.

Vivian lived there – in the 'connection house', as she called it – with other Nigerian women who sold sex to pay for their trip to Libya, just like her. Afterwards, the plan was to raise more money to pay for smugglers to get them across the sea to Italy. Some of Vivian's clients were Libyan men, but most of them were migrants themselves, from Gambia, Ghana, Senegal and Ivory Coast. They were either men who, like her, saw Libya as a stopover on the way to Europe, or they considered Libya their final destination and were hired labourers hoping for more work in the wake of the fall of Gaddafi.

I try to figure out more precisely where in Libya Vivian's brothel was located. She calls one of the women who worked there with her, because she has forgotten what the town was called. 'Tajoura,' she tells me. 'That was where I lived. That's where the brothel was.'

While writing this book, I realise that name sounds familiar for another reason so I google it. Tajoura is twenty-three kilometres east of Tripoli, on the coast. It is also the front line for rival Libyan factions; a place where one faction dropped a bomb on an overfilled detention centre and killed fifty-two migrants who were being held there in 2019. In the city, there is a large cemetery surrounded by cliffs and trees for the drowned migrants who wash up on the beach and are buried with a number instead of a name. This is why I had heard of the place before. This was not just a quiet little town. Vivian's brothel was in one of the most talked-about migration cities in Libya.

The men who visited the brothel could choose 'short time' sex – an hour for two to five US dollars,[25] depending on the service, or 'long time' sex – a whole night for 15 US dollars.[26] Vivian had mostly short-time clients, one or two per day.

'How did you feel about the work?' I asked.

'I didn't like it. Not at all. It didn't seem right for me. But I didn't have a choice. I had nothing else to offer and I had sworn to pay back Tony when I made it to Libya. That's why I say I was trafficked to Libya, but not against my will. And I had given Tony some hair I cut off from my head, my armpits and down low. So if I didn't pay him back, I was afraid that Ayelala would punish me. That is a spirit who can possess things, so you could get hit by a scooter that Ayelala possessed. My uncle is an Ayelala priest. That's common in Benin City.'

I tell Vivian about the last time I was in Nigeria, when Becky and Chika took me to visit an Ayelala temple. The female witch doctor, as she called herself, showed us several objects she used in her ceremonies: snakeskin, dried bird corpses and a stone about the size of a fist, which she said that Ayelala could drop from the sky to kill someone who had sinned. The priest explained that Ayelala is the god of justice. According to the legend, she was an enslaved woman who was going to be sacrificed in an adultery case. But just before she was to be killed, she yelled out, 'Ayelala, the world is terrible!'

'Yes,' says Vivian, nodding. 'We call on Ayelala when we need truth and justice, because she punishes lies

[25] 1–4 GBP
[26] 11 GBP

and dishonesty. The difference between God and Ayelala is that you might have to wait a long time for God to do something, but Ayelala can bring punishment immediately. But anyway, after coming to Italy, I don't believe in Ayelala any more. I've read the bible here, and I've been to church, and I know that you can only have one God.' A bit apologetically, she adds, 'So I don't believe in anything except God.'

Prison

One day, while Vivian was living at the brothel in Tajoura, there was a terrible fight in the building between a group of migrant men, and the Libyan police stormed the place and chased everyone out. A few got away, but most of them were put in migrant prison, including Vivian.

On the day we talk about prison, we are drinking espresso and eating Nutella croissants at a roadside cafe on the outskirts of Syracuse.

'I was in prison in Libya,' says Vivian. 'The prison guards tried to rape us constantly. They hit us, *mamma mia*, so our skin was black and blue all over.' She whacks her thigh and pretends to hit the side of her head. 'I was not raped in prison; that happened later. But there was a war going on in Libya, so sometimes there were chances to escape from prison – for example, if there was a bombing nearby. One day, the prison was totally quiet, as if everyone had left. There were still fences all around, but no guards. I don't know why. We waited for a while, sitting and listening, but we couldn't hear any guards. So I ran with three other women and we crawled over the fence. It was high, but two young men helped us. They were escaping too and they helped us over.

'The two men led us to an apartment where other Nigerians were living too. We were tired and happy to have escaped from prison. When the four of us women had settled down to sleep in our room, the men that fled with us came in and wanted to have sex. They said, "We helped you escape, so now you do something for us."' Vivian looks at me and gives a sarcastic laugh. 'Nothing is free,' she says. 'We told them, "We can do it tomorrow when you are done with work." But we took off before they got home.

'I still owed Tony money and now I didn't have a job. I couldn't go back to the brothel that was raided and Tony was after me. He was pressuring me to pay my debt. He was all over me.' She puts her hand to her throat. 'One of my clients repaid most of my debt for me, 1,000 dinar.[27] He bought me so he could have sex with me every night. I sort of became his wife. He was from Ghana and actually very nice. But he always had a lot of women in his connection house and he gave me an STD.

'Another Ghanaian man I knew said that he could get me a job as a maid for a Libyan family. I said yes and moved to the coastal city of Zuwara. I lived there for two years with a lively Libyan family and paid back the rest of my debt to Tony. It took me about eight months in total. I really liked the wife, but the husband, a Libyan policeman, often hit her. I could hear it at night. I think he hit her because she wouldn't have sex with him. I did their laundry and a lot of her panties were torn up.

'One day, the whole family was out and I was cleaning the house. Afterwards, I got washed up and was walking around the empty house with a towel around me. It was rare that I was home alone. I walked into the room I shared with the children to get dressed. Suddenly, the husband was there in the children's room. He grabbed me from behind, threw me down

[27] 138 GBP

on the children's mattresses and raped me. I felt so horrible after that. I felt ashamed and I had to look at his face every morning, make food for him, clean up after him, wash his dirty clothes, his underwear. I couldn't stand it.

'I packed my bags and left. I left behind a note to his wife, telling her that I had the chance to return to Nigeria and see my kids. She believed me and was glad for me, but also sad that I left. I never told her that her husband raped me. They are still married.

'Now I was unemployed again, but I got in touch with a new brothel and found work there. That is where I earned the rest of the money to cross the Mediterranean. They advertised that they had a beautiful new girl – that was me.' Vivian looks embarrassed. 'But they always did that when a new girl arrived. "Come try our new girl."'

Suddenly, she asks me, 'Are you writing all this down?'

'Yes, I'm writing down everything you say.'

'Well, anyway, it was at that brothel that I met Kindys' father. He wasn't a client, but his friend was. He came by frequently and sat on the sofa at the entrance of the brothel and looked at me when I came out to bring clients into the bed. And he was still there when we came out. One day, he told the owner that he didn't want me to have any more clients, that he wanted to take me with him. I said that I wouldn't go with him unless he paid – "You don't get a night for free." So he paid for our first night, 70 dinars.[28] After that, we became real girlfriend and boyfriend and I stopped working at the brothel.

[28] 10 GBP

'But I didn't have a job, so we had to live off his income and it was difficult. Black people get paid poorly in Libya. After a few months, I got pregnant and I didn't realise it until it was too late for a legal abortion. In Libya, it's almost impossible to get an abortion unless you are wealthy and know where to go. So we had to keep the baby. But my boyfriend said from the start that I should cross the sea before the baby was born. Otherwise, bombings in Libya would kill the baby, or life would be so hard in Libya that he wouldn't be able to take care of us. He said he would leave me if I didn't cross the sea. But I didn't want to leave with a baby inside me; the journey scared me already. In the months my baby was growing inside me, it was getting more and more difficult to walk on the street in Tajoura. Young boys threw stones at me when I went shopping and yelled racial slurs at me. There was military everywhere. We could hear explosions day and night. I started to think that my boyfriend was right, that I should cross the sea with my baby inside me, that it would be safer than carrying an infant and safer than staying in Libya. My aunt, who was already in Italy, said she thought they would let me stay in Italy if I arrived pregnant.

'With every week that passed, I felt more and more pressure to leave, as if my life's last chance was to make it to Europe. But at the same time, I didn't want to leave on just any boat. My boyfriend knew some people who sailed people over and we thought I would go with them. But they didn't go every day. They had three boats, but they only left when enough people had paid for the trip, several hundred people, I had heard. So I had to wait until the boats were ready.

I paid 2,400 dinars[29] in advance, which was the money I had earned at the brothel. That was my entire savings, so I would be arriving in Europe with no money. But I thought the price was high because we would be taking one of the big boats, a kind of ferry. So I waited, hoping that I wouldn't give birth before we left.'

[29] 330 GBP

Rescue

Vivian was in her ninth month of pregnancy when she boarded an old blue wooden boat the night of 5 April 2015. In calm weather, they set off into the Mediterranean towards Europe. 'They pushed us,' says Vivian, explaining how her journey over the sea began. The boat set out from Tajoura, where Vivian had arrived three years earlier to work at a brothel.

'Even though I lived in Tajoura, I didn't know exactly which boats they used; there were so many different kinds. For a couple of days, I stayed in one of the houses where people wait before they are taken all the way out to the coast on the night of departure. When I went down to the beach in the dark and saw the three boats that were going to sail that night, I said to one of the others, "Is that what I paid all this money for?" It wasn't a modern ferry at all. I was scared just looking at the boat. I was sure that we were all going to die. But once you've paid, you can't turn back. You won't get your money back. My boyfriend was on the beach. He said that I had to cross the sea now and that he would come later.

'I knew two young Nigerian men who were going in the same boat and I asked them to help me. They each took my arm and helped my heavy body onto the boat, and they sat on either side of me. Otherwise, I didn't know anyone on the boat. Most of them thought that one of these young men was my boyfriend.

'Before we left, the people who were running the

boat told us the rules: "1. No food on board. 2. No mobile phones, because the coastguard can detect us. 3. For women menstruating, keep your blood inside! It attracts big fish if you fall in the water."'

'Did they really say that?' I interrupted.

'Yes, that's what they said.'

I said, 'Maybe they meant sharks.'

Vivian shrugs her shoulders, as if she knows it sounds crazy that big fish might come and eat menstruating women because they smelled the blood. She continues, '"4. Never change sides in the boat. We have to stay where we are, regardless of the waves, because if you all move to one side, the boat will tip." I put my mobile phone in my bra, so they couldn't see it.

'We were the first of the three ships to sail. I think there were 2,500 people divided between the three boats. There were two levels, one below sea level and one above. It was blue with white stripes. I sat on the upper deck between the two men. People applauded when we left the shore because they were happy we were finally on our way and the water was still calm. The one guy next to me who I talked to the most massaged my belly and said he could feel the baby kicking. He was really sweet. After a little while, the boat started to rock and I got seasick and threw up. He helped me turn around so I could throw up over the railing. But it was hard to kneel with my big belly and throw up without being tossed around. There were more and more waves the further we went out. It was pitch black now and we couldn't see the two boats behind us. I thought it was good when the boats were sailing together; it felt comforting that we were so many people. But our boat was alone in the dark now. People were throwing up. It was horrible. People were throwing up on each other because we were packed in so tight, almost on top of each other. The ones who threw up the most went all slack and just swayed with the boat, swallowing their vomit. The boat went up against the waves and we went crooked, and some people rolled down and landed hard at the bottom of the boat between the waves. At each wave, more water spilled in over the railing and down into the lower level, where people were sitting. Some people began bailing with buckets and tossing water overboard, but they couldn't keep up. The two men kept sitting beside me, one holding my belly. The baby was still kicking. Suddenly, the motor stopped. There was only the noise of the waves and people shouting. No motor noise. We were being tossed by the waves with no control over the direction. I told the men that it was time to say our prayers. "Say your last prayer," I said. "We don't know what's going to happen now." My entire body was tense.

'I think we rolled around the sea for several hours. People were hanging over the railing and over each other. It was starting to get light out and two big ships sailed towards us, and then past us. They didn't care about us. A helicopter came and shone a light on us, and flew away again. I thought we wouldn't get saved. They didn't seem to care.

'Then one of the large fishing boats I had seen in Libya came close up to us, threw us a rope and towed us along. When we entered Italian waters, they cut the rope and turned around. But there were Italian coastguard ships waiting there. The coastguard arrested the fishermen who towed our boat and then took us on board their ship. The two boats we had left with were gone. I don't know what happened to them. I cried with relief when we were on the coastguard ship and were sailed into land. They checked my baby's heartbeat and they said that I was OK. Then they drove me to the refugee camp. I haven't seen those two men since. But I heard that one is in Palermo and the other one is in Germany. Twelve days later, I gave birth to Kindys.'

The Unidentified

Sicily, 2017

I research what happened to the other two boats that Vivian talked about, the ones that didn't land with them. I google the news from that period and I check the UN and EU updates about migration and shipwrecks. Maybe they landed somewhere else or were forced to return to Libya. I can't find anything about a shipwreck on 6 April 2015. I can see in the files that several thousand people arrived in Italy in the days following, so perhaps all three boats made it.

But I can also see that over a hundred people washed up on the coast of Tajoura in the following days. They found several women and children among the dead, who were then buried at the migrant cemetery in the city.

While I am researching this, I reread an article about twenty-six young Nigerian women and girls who were found dead on 5 November 2017 by a rescue boat in the open sea. Some of the few survivors, who were found on a capsized rubber boat nearby, said that the women had left on boats from Libya, but were originally from Benin City in Nigeria. Shortly thereafter, two men – an Egyptian and a Libyan – were arrested for people smuggling.

The burial of the women was paid for by Italian authorities and received massive international media coverage. NGO activists, Italian and international media, local politicians and Nigerian sex workers in

Italy participated in the funeral, which appeared on the front page of *The New York Times*. Journalists wrote that the women were sex slaves – victims of trafficking – on their way to Europe. That is common. Migrant women usually only get attention when they are called sex slaves, drowning in large numbers in the Mediterranean, or selling sex on the street.

A Nigerian woman sent me a photo from the funeral ceremony in Salerno. The caskets of the twenty-six women were placed in a row on a stone podium with a single white rose atop each one. Only two of the deceased Nigerian women could be identified. They were both pregnant.

I drive out to one of the cemeteries where migrants who drowned in the sea are buried. At the entrance to the cemetery, a group of older men is sitting under the shade of a tree. It is two o'clock and the Sicilian sun is bright. It turns out that the men are gravediggers. I explain my errand and one of the men stands up to show me the way. We walk past large marble monuments that resemble small houses, inside of which there are urns on shelves and photos of the deceased. In front of several of them, family members are sitting and chatting on folding chairs. On the graves we pass, there are names and flowers or decorations.

'Here lie the poor of the city,' says the gravedigger, pointing at a plot of land to our left. 'These people couldn't afford a funeral and a big gravesite.' The government pays for these sites. The ground is untended and there are small stones with names on them dug into the ground. There are flowers on some of them.

We walk a bit further. 'Here it is,' he says. We are standing before a large, uneven plot of ground. The

The funeral of Nigerian women after a shipwreck on the Mediterranean.

earth is cracked from drought, with weeds sticking up. The little white blooms of the weeds are the only flowers here.

Every metre, there is a black rod with a little metal plate on the end. The gravedigger says, 'We write on there what we know about the person who was found in the sea.' He points to one metal plate that reads, 'Nave: Sofia Reina 21/07/2016. S: Femminile.' He explains how to interpret it: 'This is a woman who was found at the ship *Sofia Reina* on 21 July 2016.' There are hundreds of plates like these, some with more data because there may be several deceased in the same grave.

Some of the graves are from another catastrophe, which occurred on 18 April 2015 when more than 800 people drowned on an overfilled wooden boat. The survivors were brought to land in Sicily, where they said that a third of the passengers were women and children, sitting below for protection against the cold. But when the boat capsized, they got trapped. When the boat had started to take on water, the passengers on deck tried to get the attention of passing ships and they rushed to one side. The ship tipped over because they were trying to get rescued.

That day, 18 April 2025, is mostly forgotten, but in many ways this catastrophe became Ground Zero for the European refugee crisis. It was the deadliest shipwreck in the Mediterranean to date, involving 1,100 people from more than 20 countries. Only 28 survived.

That blue wooden ship had launched from Tajoura, the same place where Vivian's ship left twelve days before. Vivian could have been lying here in the cemetery nameless, with Kindys in her belly.

The gravedigger explains to me what happens to

Vivian and Kindys were rescued on the Mediterranean. More than 30,000 people have gone missing at sea in the past ten years

the bodies of migrants recovered from the sea. The search and rescue ships in the Mediterranean bring the migrants into harbour at Catania or another port. Both dead and alive. The corpses are brought to a mortuary where they are examined for documents and personal belongings. The belongings are kept at an office, in case family members come looking for them. Sixty-five per cent of the migrants who drown on the European border remain unidentified.

I think about the many families I met in Nigeria who have lost a loved one on their way to Europe, or who didn't know if they were dead or alive. At some point, the phone stopped ringing and they wondered what had happened to them. Migrants may be unknown strangers here, but they aren't unknown to someone.

On the other side of the cemetery, across from the migrant burial ground, separated by a small tarmac path, lie ornate Italian graves with names and flowers. Borders remains in death. I brought a small white flower with me to the cemetery, not knowing what I would see. None of the graves here have flowers. I walk to the centre of the burial ground and set my flower on a sandhill, which might be a grave.

Mr Andrew and Mr Scott

Zambia, 2018

In the taxi on the way to Copenhagen Airport, the driver asks where I'm going.

'I'm on the way to Zambia to trace my family. My grandparents went there to find work in the 1950s,' I say.

He is Danish–Pakistani and his face lights up. 'Did Danes migrate to find work?' he asks, and while the taxi speeds through Amager, I tell the story of my grandfather, who saw an ad in the newspaper for mineworkers needed in Africa. So now my family and I are travelling to Zambia to find the place where they lived. My father hasn't been there since they left more than sixty years ago.

'That is just like my parents,' says the driver. 'My father saw an ad in the newspaper in Pakistan back in the 1970s. He found work in a paint factory in Valby, and lived in an apartment with eight men from the same Pakistani village. Later, my mother followed with us children. But they moved back to Pakistan after forty years in Denmark. They built a house with the money that my father earned here.'

We cheerfully recite the similarities between our Danish and Pakistani families. They went from being unemployed to being migrant workers. From being renters to owners. They worked hard and were homesick. They were worried about their children and raising them far from the culture of their homeland. They took chances to create a better life.

'They are identical stories,' says the driver with a friendly chuckle.

'Yes, in a way,' I say, hesitantly. I know that migration does not turn out the same way for everyone.

We have planned this trip for years, almost since I was a child. Now we are on our way. My father, his wife Kirsten and I. We arrive in northern Zambia, the Copperbelt, near the border of the Democratic Republic of the Congo. Here is where thousands of tons of copper were dug from the mines in the 1950s to the 1970s, to be used in European and American telephone cables.

We drive first to Mufulira, a city whose name I heard as a child. There are tall trees with gorgeous crowns along the main road through the city. The dirt in the gardens is red. White colonial buildings, where European families once lived, are now used for government offices and schools.

We drive out to the Slave Tree located in Ndola, under whose shade slave traders gathered and bound their slaves before selling them. A group of young men is standing beneath the tree. They stare at us. Not many tourists come here. It is hard to read what it says on the metal plate on the tree, but we can make out that the British banned slavery at the start of the 1800s. Today, the old mahogany tree is a termite-ridden memorial to all those who lost their lives as enslaved people.

In the city's mine archives, we look through dusty newspapers for news from the period that my father was here. On the cover of several magazines, Queen Elizabeth is pictured on a horse. There is good advice for the white European housewives about how to get rid of fleas and lice in the new mineworker houses. In the cinema, they are showing the new Elvis films, which my father remembers seeing.

We drive past a marketplace on the edge of the city, where women are sitting on the rocky ground selling vegetables, with their children on their laps.

And there it is, the mine, with a high fence around it and enormous steel supports that criss-cross in what appears to me to be an incomprehensible structure, like a being that lifts copper from the earth's abyss. There are almost no people, as only a few parts of the mine are still operational.

Equipped with an old city map from 1961, we search near the mine for my father's childhood home – the house where Grandma Ella sat in her chair by the crocheted tablecloth. We find the house: number 7A. It looks like the old pictures my father has, though the windows are peeling and several roof tiles are missing, replaced with black plastic bags. A couple of children are running around playing and a dog is barking. We stand at the edge of the yard, looking. A young woman notices us and comes over with a child on her hip. We explain who we are and why we came. That we don't mean to intrude. But the family is very welcoming and invites us inside. Mr Andrew, a Zambian, lives here with his grown daughters and his grandchildren.

Mr Andrew also worked in the mine, but lost both his legs to diabetes. Now, he lives in his bed in front of the TV, all day and night, in the bedroom that once was my grandparents'. A dusty wheelchair stands in a corner. Mr Andrew is sitting in the same room, the same bed, where my grandmother once lay, homesick for Denmark and for her family in Ringkøbing.

We show Mr Andrew pictures of his house the way it looked in the 1950s. The house is what we have in common. We compare how it looked then to how it looks now, noting the large cracks in the walls and holes in the floor that have appeared over time. My father recognises from his childhood some of the pieces of furniture that my grandparents left behind when they left for Denmark. They are still there in the living room.

My father is back in his childhood universe for the first time in sixty years. It is overwhelming to imagine that he ran around here and played as a boy on these dusty red roads. He seems a bit self-conscious and is soon ready to leave.

We drive off, talking in the car about the strong feelings that come up when one's childhood, with all its mystique, is reduced to a little dilapidated house. And there is another layer of emotion on top of that. My grandparents bought their terraced house in Emdrup, but while the Anglo American Corporation earned billions extracting copper from Africa, what did Mr Andrew and the Zambians get out of the Zambian copper mines? Mr Andrew is getting by because his daughter is a migrant in South Africa and sends money home.

We drive out to the former mine Bwana Mkubwa, where we know my grandfather also worked. He was a labourer there for a long time and they lived in a house in the bush before they got the little red mineworker's house. An older, white South African, Mr Scott, is sitting inside a run-down office. The mine has shut down, but every bit has to be sold and Mr Scott is counting on the Congo and China as buyers. As in Nigeria, the Chinese are making inroads where the Europeans left. The now-laid-off Zambian mineworkers are getting nothing from the sale of the mine. 'All that's left is me and the black tea boy,' says Mr Scott, pointing at the young boy in the corner, holding a tray. Did he just say black 'tea boy' without blinking an eye?

The Monument

Sicily, 2019

We're on the beach in Sicily – Vivian, Kindys, my children and I. Everyone is in the water except for Vivian. She is sitting in the sand, her feet in the water, wearing the swimming costume she borrowed from me.

'Don't you want to come in the water?' I ask her.

'I can't swim,' she says. Kindys walks hesitantly out into the warm water. He is four now and has never been swimming before. He wants his mother with him and he convinces her to sit in my daughter's float ring. Vivian splashes around in the shallow water, holding Kindys' hand.

'Do you ever think about how you crossed that sea?' I ask her.

'No, I don't think of it like that; it's not my sea. I can't think about it. It was just how I got here.'

The next day, I walk along the beach looking out over the sea, blue and calm in the sunshine. I meander to the Monumento ai Caduti italiani d'Africa, not far from Vivian's refugee centre in Syracuse. It is a stone and bronze monument in the shape of the prow of a ship on its way across the Mediterranean, erected during the Fascist era under Mussolini. Uniformed Italian soldiers in bronze with rifles, a broad-shouldered airman holding a bomb and a tank engraved in stone are in memory of the Italians who crossed the Mediterranean and died during the colonisation of Ethiopia in the 1930s. 'The northern front' and 'The southern front' are engraved on it. Between the two fronts is the Mediterranean Sea. The monument is placed here because Syracuse was the centre for soldiers embarking to fight for the colonisation of Africa. Today, Syracuse receives African migrants who are sailing in the opposite direction, across the Mediterranean in dilapidated boats.

Couples are sitting and kissing on the benches around the monument. A man is speaking loud Italian into his mobile phone as he looks out over the sea. I climb the three big steps to the top of the monument and lean against the wall with the sun in my face. It is both a work day and a day off. It's often like that here. My thoughts keep making connections. I am not just thinking of the Mediterranean as the place of my childhood holidays, or of the calm waves and the sparkling sunsets. When I look over the Mediterranean, I see the ocean as a cemetery, a political zone and a place for research. The sea is a deadly border between Africa and Europe.

I lay my mobile flat on the hot stone, in the same direction as the prow of the monument, pointing out towards the water. I open the compass app. The needle points directly at Tajoura, from where Vivian left. I get a feeling in the pit of my stomach: Vivian's life, her trip and now the compass needle, pointing directly from the place where she arrived in Europe back to the place she left in Africa, then on to Ethiopia, right into the history of colonisation.

If I turn the compass one centimetre, it points right at Zambia's copper mines, where my grandfather earned money for the house in Emdrup.

My Tomorrow Must Be Greater Than Today

I wake up in Vivian's room to the sound of gospel music. At the new refugee centre where she lives, Vivian is in the bed across from me, looking into her phone and singing along. 'No matter what I face, no matter what I see, no matter what comes my way, no matter how I cry . . . One thing I know, that is definite in my heart, my tomorrow must be greater than today.' Behind her, Kindys is sleeping. It's early, but the dry Sicilian sun is already up, flickering through the room's wooden shutters.

Vivian gets out of bed, puts down her mobile and keeps singing while she washes. It was a late night. Vivian made Nigerian chicken in spinach, together with her friend Mary and me, and she asked if I would sleep over in her room. She enjoys having me over to eat, sleep and go with her to church. She likes having me as a guest, as a friend, while she is more than just a research subject to me, more than just someone who needs help understanding documents. She finds a clean towel in the cupboard and says that I can wash too. She has a private bathroom because she has Kindys. There is a pair of worn high-heeled shoes on the radiator in the bathroom and Vivian's shiny wigs with smooth, black hair hang on the towel hooks. The door doesn't close all the way and while I wash, I can hear Vivian singing some more.

Later, we drink instant coffee, wake Kindys, eat toast

and wash up the plates and pans from dinner the night before in the communal kitchen.

Vivian puts on a tight, red dress, sandals with heels and long, sparkling earrings. On our way out, we have to pass a little room where the nuns who run the centre work. One of them asks Vivian why she is wearing that dress again, while staring at me pointedly, as if she would like validation from me in return. I shrug my shoulders. Vivian laughs, 'I'm going to church. I have it on for God's sake.'

When we are out on the street, I ask, 'Why did she ask you about your dress?'

She replies, 'They're worried about how I earn money, that I'm getting it from men. So they always ask about my clothes and where I'm going, and where I get my money. They say they're afraid that other people will think I'm with men and that I'm immoral.'

Vivian got the chicken we ate the day before from a young Nigerian man, who received her phone number in return. We were at the market and she turned and looked me in the eyes. 'Now, pay attention, Sine,' she said. 'This is how I survive.'

When the young man asked for her number, she answered, flirtatiously, 'If you want my phone number, you have to buy me something.' He followed her through the market to a stall. She selected a large yam, spinach, a frozen chicken and three cans of tomato sauce. He paid, she gave him her number and it appeared as if this had been more expensive than he had planned. 'He wants to be my boyfriend,' she said. 'But he's too young. I need someone who has a job.'

Vivian is currently a dishwasher at a tourist resort

outside the city, where she earns 500 euros[30] per month, working seven days a week from 7 a.m. to 8 p.m. Over lunch, Vivian and her co-worker Mary commented, as if it was self-evident, that you make more money selling sex and trading your phone number for food than you do washing tourists' plates. Italian men pay 50 euros[31] for sex. Nigerian, Ghanian and Libyan men pay 20 euros.[32] For the most part, Vivian limits herself to phone numbers and flirting.

She shows me a photo of a white man. 'He's from Denmark,' she says. 'Do you know him?' I look at the photo and shake my head. He has blond hair and is heavy-set, and lives in Sjælland. She has chatted with him a bit on the dating site Afro-Introductions.com, where she and several of her friends have profiles. They write that they are vibrant African women, they show their long, braided hair, mention their 'African bums' and dance alluringly in short livestream videos. On this website, thousands of Italian and other white European men search for African women. Some of the women mention in their profiles that they have children, while others do not. The men Vivian is in contact with don't seem to mind that she has three children: two in Nigeria and Kindys in Italy.

'Can't you find a nice husband for me?' she asks. 'If I don't find a husband soon, I will let myself be smuggled in the boot of a car through the mountains to France. There should be more work there.'

I tell her I will think about possible husbands. She says, 'Don't think, Sine. Find me a husband!'

[30] 433 GBP
[31] 43 GBP
[32] 17 GBP

12 + 5

Later, we meet Mary at a little bakery not far from the camp. We order pizza and drinks for lunch. While I am paying, Vivian and Mary are whispering intensely by a refrigerator filled with cold drinks. Something is wrong. I ask what they're talking about. Vivian gives Mary a look, an I'm-going-to-tell-her look. 'Mary's pregnant,' she says. 'But the nuns at the camp won't help her. They say abortion is a sin. But she's been pregnant for a while now and when the people at the hotel see it, they'll fire her.'

Mary wants to have an abortion. She has only had the dishwashing job for two months and she can't take care of another child. She is already sending money to her four children in Nigeria. 'I did not plan to have another baby,' she says. 'It's because of my job.' I ask if I can try to help her.

We take the bus to the hospital. There is a queue and I knock vigorously on the doors and say that Mary needs help. It's an emergency. We are sent to a clinic on the edge of the city for a scan. Mary takes off her trousers and crawls up on the bed behind a screen. I can hear the heartbeat and see the foetus. Mary says, '*Mamma mia*. Forgive me.' The older male doctor says that she is over twelve weeks along. She is twelve weeks and five days and he turns down her request for an abortion. In Italy, the limit is twelve weeks.

'But it is still twelve weeks, in a way,' I say.

'No,' says the doctor flatly. 'It is twelve weeks and five days.'

We walk slowly down the clinic steps. I am overwhelmed by a feeling of helplessness about Mary's life becoming even more chaotic than it already is; that a baby will be born to a mother who can't deal with it. I feel angry.

We sit down on a bench and eat our pizza leftovers. Mary says hello to a Nigerian couple with a child who are on their way up to the doctor. Then we return to the refugee centre.

We sit on Mary's bed, not knowing what we're waiting for. An hour later, I get a text from the hospital. 'Come with the patient tomorrow at 7 a.m., fasting.' It's from the nurse we met earlier in the day, the one who sent us to the doctor. Evidently, she was able to work around the system. Mary calls Vivian. 'They're going to do it for me,' she says. 'They're doing it.'

After she hangs up, she turns to me and says, 'If I hadn't been there with a white person, they wouldn't have paid me any attention. It's like black women are invisible.'

The next morning, I say goodbye to Mary at the hospital entrance. She walks to the gynaecology department and has her abortion. Then she returns to her life: mother to four children in Nigeria, illegal immigrant, dishwasher and occasional sex worker in Sicily.

Abortion, Abortion, Abortion

My notebooks are filled with abortions, births, dead women and dead babies. Rereading my notebooks and connecting the stories is overwhelming. Becky died with her baby in her belly, of relatively common birth complications, because she was unable to give birth at a decent hospital on her way to Europe. There was no one to remove the dead baby from her. Lek had a foetus aborted in the seventh month. Vivian aborted her dissolved baby over the toilet. Lom had an abortion at an illegal clinic in Bangkok. And Mary barely got hers in time.

But an abortion is not just an abortion. I had an abortion in hospital in Viborg when I was sixteen. My mother arranged the appointment and two days later, I was lying in a gynaecological ward. The doctor said, 'When I give you this shot, it's the point of no return. Are you sure you want to do this?' I said yes and I thought it sounded so dramatic. I woke up in a room with other women who were either trying not to lose their pregnancies or who had just given birth. My teenage boyfriend came and brought me flowers.

Even though I cried, even though one night I looked up at the starry sky and thought about that life I had removed, and even though sometimes I still calculate how old that child would be now if I had kept it, that free, legal and safe abortion allowed me to return to my life again as a sixteen-year-old.

The women I am writing about have removed their

foetuses with soapy water injections; herbal mixtures; a poisonous cocktail of alcohol, chilli, bark and herbs; boiling hot water in their uterus; pills; injections from people without a medical education; sharp instruments inside their uterus, with horrible complications, bleeding and infections. Sex workers know something about how to get rid of a pregnancy when no one else will help you. And their knowledge is a harsh look into a reality where women do not have access to legal abortion and have to find their own solutions.

Women's abortions are all different, but they are often evidence of the consequences of having limited say over your own body when you are a woman without access to birth control, have no money and are undocumented, or live in a country without access to legal abortion.

Abortion and sex work are not just connected because abortion is a work hazard, but also because both are areas in which governments, religions and all kinds of other people – men, families, employers – want to control women's bodies. Behind the opposition to decriminalising abortion and sex work lies the belief that women, perhaps sex workers in particular, are unfit to make decisions about their own bodies.

It is estimated that in Nigeria, there are 500,000 unsafe abortions every year and abortions are the cause of 40 per cent of the nation's extremely high maternal mortality rate, one of the highest in the world.[xvii]

Still, Vivian would rather talk about being a sex worker than about having a second abortion in Sicily a few years ago. She is ashamed of it. Shame and blame follow the women, even though their pregnancies are almost always because of their work, their lack of access to birth control, their unemployment, their inability to track their cycle, men who demand sex without a condom, their absentee husbands who won't support another child or a government that prohibits abortion.

Just as an abortion is not just an abortion, a birth is not just a birth. I think of the women in Denmark, and in other places, who are returning to home births, the idea of the 'natural' birth – the romantic ideal of birth as an authentic, homey, intimate experience. I wanted that for Ella's birth. But it was good that I didn't do it, because it might have killed me. When I was pregnant with Wilder, my fourth child, and I talked about this with my older midwife, who had attended thousands of births, she said dryly, 'Births are about safety; save your experiences for the amusement park.'

I think of all the migrant women and sex workers that I have met through my work, who can only dream of being able to give birth safely in a hospital. What a difference: the possibility to choose one or the other, as opposed to having no choice. What a vulnerable situation, not to be able to get the help you need when the baby or the foetus in your uterus needs to come out, dead or alive.

Vivian, Lom, Becky, Sommai and I all remember where, how, when and with whom we had our abortions. And, except for Becky, who had no children, with whom we gave birth. And none of us has regretted either our children or our abortions. We decided not to have the children we couldn't take care of and we decided to have the children we could. Vivian says that she does sometimes regret having to say no to better-paying jobs and night work. And a person might regret having children after long nights with a screaming baby, or when it prevents you from pursuing some possibility. But at the same time, you love them and regret nothing. It is all true at the same time.

Kids, Kids, Kids

'I don't know if I should offer congratulations,' one of my family members said when I became pregnant with my first child, Julius, in 1996. It was the year after I graduated from secondary school. People thought I was too young, obviously. I was nineteen when I became pregnant, but both his father and I wanted him.

The first night at the national hospital with my newborn, Julius, I shared a room with a woman who had given birth to her second child. We sat in the dark, nursing our babies, and she said, 'When I had my first son, I learned that there is only one person in the world I would die for, and that is my child.' She paused and went on, 'But I think my husband thinks that I would also die for him.' She chuckled.

In the hospital bed in the dark, with Julius in my arms, I didn't grasp the enormity of what she had said. That she would die for her child; that she would disappear so her child could go on living. It was as if she was speaking about something completely foreign, a new world that did not yet include me. I saw in my mind a car about to run over a child and the woman jumping in front to save it and being killed herself.

In time, my baby taught me something else. It wasn't about throwing myself in front of a car. It was the all-consuming sense that if a child dies, then part of oneself dies too. You know that the ruination of your own life is right there, like an abyss, if your child dies.

To feel that you would die for your child means that you give over your mental well-being to another and let your heart go around in the world unprotected. It means providing for and supporting your child, giving him or her the best possible circumstances from the resources that you have to offer. And however crazy it may feel, that you are responsible for another person and that you will endure pain and a bad conscience if you are not able to give them what they need.

I was only twenty when Julius was born, but I lived in Denmark and I didn't think that a child would impede my future at all. I could apply for extra government support as a parent and receive a daycare spot at a very low price. My child was taken care of while I studied for my degree. The social safety-net held me.

Sex work and love rarely occur in the same sentence or in the same story. But they are inextricably interwoven. One of the biggest differences between male and female migrants is that the women have uteruses, and this biological fact determines their fate.

This is no rosy picture of mothers who will give up everything: the self-sacrificing mother. This is a complex love. Their sex work is deeply connected to their love for their children. It is deeply connected to the necessity and duty of taking care of their children, as parents do.

Sex work is a commodity, but in complex human accounting it is also a gift of love – not to the client, but to the child and to the family back home; to not only maintain their family's life but to better it, often significantly.

Sex worker. Mother. Daughter. Woman. Worker. Their lives encompass all of these roles.

The Woman War

Sicily, 2019

Vivian puts on her backpack and places Kindys in the pushchair. On the walk from the camp to the city centre, we pass the monument with the soldiers facing Africa and, later, a Madonna cross with plastic flowers, as we rattle through the dilapidated park with the pushchair's plastic wheels.

'The other day,' says Vivian, 'I found a snake here. It was just like the ones we have in the village in Nigeria. But I killed it right away ... I hate snakes! It didn't know a Nigerian woman was passing by, poor thing.' She laughs loudly. It reminds me of Becky's laugh.

Vivian has been summoned to the police station because, she says, they want to take her fingerprints. Since she crossed the Mediterranean, her life has been about being patient: fingerprintings, questionings and insecurity about how long she will be allowed to stay in Italy. We wait on white plastic chairs inside the beautiful but run-down building of the border police. There are about twenty migrants waiting, most of them young men.

But the police did not summon Vivian for fingerprinting. She misunderstood. I am sitting with Kindys on my lap while she finds out that she has ten days to leave Italy. Like thousands of migrants in Italy are finding out during this period, her humanitarian visa is not being extended. Whoever came with the migrant crisis has to return home. The policeman looks a bit sheepish when he tells her, 'They are especially targeting you Nigerians, I'm sorry to say.'

Vivian is shocked and she calls Mary when we get outside. 'They said I can only be here if there is war in Nigeria, but there isn't any war in Benin City. I have my private war. The Women's War. War in my family at home.'

In my notebook from that day, I write: 'You can't find refuge from the Women's War; war has many forms.'

We walk over to the city's overburdened migrant centre, which provides help for free. The lawyer there says, 'Your son is your only chance of staying in Italy. But you have to show that you're a good mother.' He wraps his two index fingers together to show a mother and child connected. 'You have to be with him all the time.'

'How can I be a good mother when I have no job and I live in a refugee camp?' asks Vivian, rhetorically. 'How the Italians define a good mother is not easy.'

Vivian and I discuss how she can prove that she's a good mother. How she can arrange her life so she can work and still spend plenty of time with Kindys. Maybe she can show the authorities some of the many loving photos of the two of them together on her phone, or maybe the drawing hanging in the camp kitchen that Kindys made in nursery. He coloured in his mother and himself with brown crayons, while all the pre-printed faces on the colouring page had white skin. 'I love you' is written on the drawing in Italian.

Vivian, the lawyer and I take a break with an espresso at the little cafe across from the migrant centre. The lawyer pours two packets of sugar in his coffee and Kindys gets a red lollipop.

We walk back to the centre's office and the lawyer

asks me to close the door, leaving Vivian outside. Vivian peers through the glass door. I shrug apologetically at her and sit down across from her lawyer. He opens his files on the computer and scrolls through hundreds of migrant cases. Vivian is one among many, but because she has Kindys, he knows her case thoroughly.

He asks me if Vivian has been a sexual victim in any way – rape, violence, trafficking? Besides Kindys being born on Italian soil, forced sexual acts are the only other thing that could help her.

'Can you help me prove it?' he asks.

The lawyer explains again that it is not enough for her to be poor, unemployed and Kindys' mother. But if there has been coercion, sex, violence, then he might be able to help. He says that if I could write an expert opinion about Vivian being a victim of rape or having been coerced into sex, it would help. I tell him, 'I'll do that.'

Stress

After the meeting with the lawyer, I walk home through the humid streets of Siracusa to my hotel, occasionally putting my hand out to lean against the walls of the houses. Back at my room, I look in the mirror. I look tired and my body feels heavy. I'm freezing cold in the room and my heart is pounding. I crawl under the covers and try to breathe deep and easy, but I lose the rhythm and toss and turn in bed for several hours. I feel sick and I realise I have been dizzy too much lately. I wonder if it's a brain tumour.

These recent days, including the intense meeting with Vivian's lawyer, have hit me hard. It is wearing on me to have spent so many years advocating for the strength and power of women, only to have to erase Vivian's power in this expert statement I have promised to write. Strong women don't get asylum.

I think about Lom, back in the hotel in Bangkok, when she asked if she shouldn't put on make-up, so she would look worse when the woman from the NGO came to check on her after her abortion and perhaps be more likely to get aid. Make-up was part of her normal day, part of her power, but she thought she would get more help if she looked weak and innocent, just imperfect skin and dark circles under her eyes, like a young girl who could be blamed for getting pregnant because she used too much make-up.

I had asked Vivian to come by later, so I could read my letter aloud to her and make sure that I got her story right. She arrives with Kindys when I am nearly finished. He starts jumping on my bed, begging to watch cartoons on my phone, because Vivian's is out of data. I give him my phone and he plays my daughter's dragon game.

I read my letter to her. 'I wrote here that you borrowed money for your trip to Libya and that you felt coerced to pay it back by selling sex. I also wrote that you left Nigeria because your ex-husband beat you and that you had no place to live. And if they don't give you asylum and you are sent home, he'll beat you again.'

'Yes, that's fine. You can write that,' Vivan says.

The next morning, we meet at the lawyer's office. I sent him my letter via email. I have to sit there for hours in a roasting hot office while the interpreter translates my letter into Italian for the lawyer. Meanwhile, he makes comments comparing what I have written with the information that Vivian gave to the authorities previously. The lights feel piercing, which the white walls only intensify. Their voices seem louder than normal. I feel dizzy and can't concentrate. I have been walking in the heat with Vivian for days and all the problems and the complex situations of these women have become a cacophony inside my head.

Everything starts to spin in the lawyer's office and I walk out to the bathroom to collect myself. I wash my face and drink some water. It doesn't help and I tell them that I have to leave because I have another meeting. Unsteady and afraid of falling, I walk slowly back to the hotel with a hand on the walls again.

When I tell people about the work I do, they often say, 'That sounds difficult! You must hear some horrible stories about sex workers, trafficking and rape.'

Sometimes I have answered that as a professional, I can keep things compartmentalised and that it doesn't feel so horrible because I know many of the women well, and have known them for so long, that I can see their lives are much more than exploitation and tragedy. They are also women with vital lives; love, birthdays, things they are in control of. Sex workers are often some of the most fun and least judgemental people to be with. Bodies, sex, love, men, money – it is all part of daily life.

But are all these years of fieldwork and listening to the women's stories finally starting to get to me and make me ill?

When I return to Copenhagen, my heart palpitations and dizziness continue. I keep feeling like I might fall and I am panicked in loud places. My heart pounds when I get a new text from Thailand, Nigeria or Thy. I don't answer right away.

I cancel a fieldwork trip to Nigeria. I would rather walk in the woods. I feel guilty. What about the women I am working with, who can't just take off and do something more enjoyable? I am often by myself, taking care of my kids, and I think that is difficult. But they have cared for their children under the most challenging conditions.

I visit my doctor, Anna, whom I have been seeing for twenty years at her clinic at an apartment in Nørrebro. 'Considering what you are working with, Sine,' she says, 'I can't believe you haven't seen me sooner ... You came here when your mother died, but otherwise you never make an appointment for anything. Maybe you need to think about yourself. How else are you going to have what it takes to do your work? Most people work thirty-seven hours a week . . . outside those thirty-seven hours, you can do things you enjoy; not go around thinking constantly about what to research, how the women are and the purpose of it all. You are allowed to take time off.'

I think Anna is right. But I don't know how to do that.

Dubai Dreams

Copenhagen, 2021

I send Lom a text from Copenhagen. 'Hey Lom, how is it going? Are you OK in Dubai? Are you working? Love, Sine.'

> Hi Love, I am actually not okay here in Dubai. There is no work and no money. I want to go back to Thailand. I have not worked in two months. Sine, you know that before Covid my life was getting better. I was earning money. I had paid off my debt and had plans to have a new roof installed on my father's house. I should have gone back to Thailand by now. Tomorrow the Thai embassy is finally opening, so we can register to return home. The problem is that people have not been working for months because everything has been closed. So they don't have money to buy plane tickets. I'm lucky because I have a place to live. I am here at the hotel with the other girls. But the freelancers have no place to live and can't earn any money. They are homeless in the streets of Dubai. I can live at the room in the hotel until the end of the month. Then I won't have a place to live either.

I send Lom 1,000 kroner[33] for the ticket to Thailand. I have her account number saved in my records and have used it often these past thirteen years that we

[33] 116 GBP

have known each other. But she ends up not flying home, because the world is starting to open up again. Clients are gradually returning to Dubai and, if she leaves, she is afraid that she won't be able to get a new visa to be able to re-enter the UAE.

Lom had been working in Dubai for four years when Covid-19 shut down the world. And she had earned a lot, often the equivalent of over £2,250 per month, ten times what she would have earned at the local Chinese-owned noodle factory in Mo Baan. Each month, she sent the equivalent of £450–£670 home to her father and her children. The rest she saved and used to cover her rent and living expenses.

After we saw each other last in 2017, when her mother died, Lom went to Pattaya and worked as a freelancer at a bar. She sent me a video from there about sending money to her father and said that he wasn't mad at her any more. But after a few months in Pattaya, she took the bus across the border to Malaysia and worked in a brothel near some of the large construction sites, where men had arrived to build Malaysia's new future, with hotels, skyscrapers and factories.

'But,' she said, 'Malaysia was too Muslim for me.' She didn't want to wear a veil or always have to be accompanied by a man outside if she didn't want to be seen as a sex worker – which she actually was. But most of all, she didn't want to stay in Malaysia because the clients almost always requested BtB – Body to Body – massages, which require a great deal more physical effort. 'Massaging clients for an hour was hard work and I was exhausted every day. I didn't want to work like that. We had no holidays and the pay was bad – less than 2,000 USD[34] per month to work seven days a week and have five or six clients per day. The only good thing was that it was cheap to take the bus to Malaysia and I didn't need a visa, so I could do it without borrowing money from anyone. So I kept all my pay and I could send money to my father and my children. I was there for ten months, but then I was able to get a visa to Dubai.'

Whatever I know about Lom's stay in Malaysia and her first four years in Dubai, during Covid and my pregnancy with Wilder, has come through our video calls on Messenger, which I then wrote in my notebooks. We hadn't seen each other for six years. But, in January 2023, I finally went to Dubai.

[34] 1,494 GBP

Al Muraqqabat

Dubai, 2023

'Can we meet right before I change my clothes?' Lom asks me on the phone. 'I can't go outside in my work clothes.'

We agree to meet on the corner by the hotel where she works, in the Al Muraqqabat neighbourhood in the old district of Dubai. Here is where migrants work at the cheap hotels, or work for wholesalers, or sell clothes, plastic items and electronics, and where many migrants also live. There is an intense and hectic energy here, from all the people coming into Dubai to do business.

Dubai is a relatively new destination on the sex industry map. At first, it was a dynamic fishing town on the Persian Gulf, then a centre for pearl diving, ship building and spice trading, where advantageous tax policies attracted Indian and Pakistani businessman in particular. But it was the discovery of oil in 1966 that truly changed the city and, in half a century, Dubai exploded into a metropolis, a jewel of global capitalism. Businessmen streamed in from across the planet and today 90 per cent of Dubai's population comes from other countries, most of them foreign workers in construction, tourism and trade. The majority are men and they arrive alone. Sixty-nine per cent of Dubai's population is male.[xviii] And women like Lom followed them.

The tourists, influencers and millionaires do not visit Al Muraqqabat when they go on luxury tours to Dubai's artificial palm tree islands and seven-star hotels. There is a hierarchy in the city based on skin colour. Women with lighter skin from Russia and Eastern Europe sell sex to the primarily white male tourists at the fancy hotels on the artificial islands. Women with brown skin, like Lom, sell sex at brothels to migrant workers who have low salaries. Nigerian women sell sex on the street at night.

Janus and my two youngest children are with me in Dubai. Wilder is still little, so I have to bring my family with me and install them in a hotel, a few hundred metres from Lom's place of work. My older children know Lom. Before she had children, she sometimes took care of Julius and Carl when I had fieldwork meetings in Thailand. Then she could get away from having clients for one night and do childcare instead. But she has never met Wilder, and Ella is six years older than when they last saw each other.

Janus and I take the kids out on the crowded streets with us so Lom can meet them.

Lom comes walking around the corner, stuffing her phone into her pocket and running towards us in her flip-flops. She gives Ella, who is ten, a big hug first, a long, motherly embrace. She left Thailand when her daughter MJ was ten and she says that she loves to hug a girl that age. She hasn't seen MJ in two and a half years and now she is nearly a teenager with a bigger body to hug. I am reminded that I have to remember to hug Ella more often, before she grows up.

Lom's hair is long and curly. She looks older now, with fine wrinkles around her eyes. She has lost weight since we sat in Mo Baan talking about her starting to sell sex again. She picks up Wilder and we give him a mutual hug between us. It feels so familiar to be together again.

We take photos of all of us with Lom in the middle and I give her the gift-wrapped, flowered black kimono that I bought for her in the airport as a present.

'I'll unwrap it at home,' she says. 'I have to get to work. It's 11 p.m., so the clients will be arriving soon.'

We agree to meet the next day and she runs off with the package under her arm to put on her work clothes and receive clients.

Now it's dark in Dubai. Wilder is in the pushchair, which Janus is pushing, and I'm walking hand in hand with Ella. Suddenly, Ella bends down and picks up a business card with a photo of a white woman in red panties, slightly pulled down over part of her arse. Her face is not visible.

'What's this, Mummy?' she asks.

I explain that the woman on the card is like the women I know and work with, and why some women do this kind of work. It is an awkward conversation to have with a girl of ten, to explain what women like Lom do and why men pay for it. I turn the card over. 'Call for sex with Russian ladies' it reads, with a phone number. Hundreds of these cards are littered on the pavement all the way back to the hotel. Dubai asserts that it forbids prostitution, according to Islamic law, but sex work is Dubai's open secret.

Later, while Lom is at work, I go with Janus and the kids to see the Burj Khalifa. It is the world's tallest building, towering over the city at 829 metres like a Tower of Babel or a gigantic phallus, with a splashing waterfall and a light show where everyone takes photos and says 'Ohhh!' while tipping their heads back to see the top.

Lom in front of the hotel in Dubai where she works

The sight of Burj Khalifa makes me think of New York City at the start of the twentieth century, when huge businesses and financial moguls competed to build the tallest building, as is happening now in Dubai. The Chrysler Building and the Empire State Building shot up to gain the public's admiration and to create excitement over what the modern world could achieve. It was a shameless celebration of power and capitalism, similar to what I see taking place in Dubai today. Right here, by the incredible heights of Burj Khalifa, it occurs to me that I am witnessing the Arab world's ultimate demonstration that it will no longer cower before the West. The tower seems to proclaim, 'We are wilder, better and faster than you. We are the future. You are the past.' Much like New York and the USA, the Arabic Emirates and Dubai are a super-charged magnetic field for migrants, yet these migrants are rarely thought of as an integral part of society. They are welcome to provide cheap labour and to be a part of the economy, but they have few rights and they have to go back home when they no longer provide value or if they create any problems.

Lom has overstayed her visa, but she says it's not a problem. She can just get a new stamp. But if she gets sick, she has to deal with it herself.

Especially if You're Pretty

The next day, Lom and I meet at Starbucks at 4 p.m., after she wakes up. Fieldwork among sex workers typically takes place no earlier than 4 p.m. and continues until they have to go to work around eleven. During this time, they can eat, have their nails and hair done, go shopping and call their families. Because of the time difference, Lom's family is about to go to bed when she wakes up in Dubai after a night of work. When she arrives, she is talking on the phone with her father. He is ready for bed after getting BM and MJ to sleep. She tells him she has arrived in Dubai and they chat about MJ and school.

We drink iced tea while we talk about her arrival in Dubai. There are some things that are hard to communicate from a distance and through a video call. I ask her, 'How did you travel to Dubai? I never quite understood that.'

She says, 'I paid an agent in Thailand 20,000 baht.[35] That paid for a tourist visa, a one-way ticket to Dubai from Bangkok and a fake return ticket. It was a direct flight, so I wouldn't be questioned in a stopover country and be sent back to Thailand. What cost the most was the 5,000 dirham[36] that I owed to the Chinese woman who ran many of the massage parlours where Thai women work here in

[35] 460 GBP
[36] 1,018 GBP

Dubai. I gave her my passport when I arrived. That's what most people do.'

'How did you feel about giving her your passport?' I ask.

'I knew I had to,' she says, as if it were obvious. 'It's illegal for them to take our passports, but they run a big risk, getting us into Dubai and then hiring us at their massage parlours without work visas. It's illegal to work on a tourist visa. Lots of people try to cheat and don't pay what they owe and they find work at hotels once they have made it into Dubai. So she holds your passport until you've paid your debt. That's their way of insuring their business. I understand. Dubai is the easiest country to enter right now, because they want tourism. And I think they also want people to come here and work . . . Even though I work illegally, the police in Dubai rarely do anything against us girls who work inside the hotels. We help each other – the hotel and "the ladies". Either the clients can come in and get a massage with extra service, or we can sit at the bar and see if we can get a client to bring us up to his room. We are extra room service for the men here. The hotel wants us, even though it is illegal to sell sex, because it's something their guests want. It's more dangerous for the ones who are standing on the street looking for clients, like the African women, because they have no one to look out for them, and the police don't want them out there. They're also racist against black people and they pick them up.'

Lom crosses her wrists, as if she has a pair of handcuffs on. 'There is more freedom when you enter on a tourist visa and then go from job to job after paying off your debt. So you have three months to pay off your debt and when it's paid off, you're free.'

'So you don't feel like you were cheated?' I ask.

'No, not me. Three months was enough time for me to pay my debt. That's enough time, especially if you're pretty.'

'If you're pretty?' I ask.

'Yes. Ugly women feel cheated. To pay off your debt fast, you have to be pretty, because the most important thing is not if you're good at giving massages, but if you're pretty. It's the clients who choose you and the clients who choose if they want extra service – that is, sex – after the massage. And if they don't think the woman is pretty, they will say no or won't leave much of a tip. So you have to be pretty to pay back your debt within three months. That's what's a shame – that the agents don't tell the ugly women they loan money to that it can be hard for them to get clients. There is competition here between all of us women, but they don't say anything about that. They make it sound like it's easy for everyone and that there is lots of work for everyone. But that's not the case. It's just like any business and the clients don't want the ugly women, unless there aren't any others.

'Sometimes, I have given a client to one of the ugly women, because my business is actually going well here. The men think I'm pretty, even though I'm older. And the ones who have come to me several times know that I am experienced. I always get them to cum. I try to pass clients to the ugly women, because they're sad and I think it's a shame for them. I tell the receptionists that they should send clients to the ugly women too. Otherwise, they can't pay off their debt.

'If they don't pay their debt within three months, they don't get their passport back and they get fired, so they have no place to work and no place to live and they still owe money. And it is hard for the ugly ones to get new jobs, because they have go in to apply and show their faces. And they can't afford to travel back home, and don't have their passports. It's a shame for them.'

I am scribbling in my notebook, again impressed by the knife-sharp market analysis and the understanding of capitalistic connections between the market, the body, desire and work, which sex workers like Lom can explain instantly over an iced tea.

Mona

A couple of days later, we are standing in a crowded market in Al Muraqqabat. Lom is looking for Vee, a woman she has heard about from the women she works with who is supposed to be good at eyelashes. Lom needs new ones, because it is easier to do her daily work make-up when her eyes are framed by long, dense lashes. 'She's from Vietnam,' Lom tells me, so I will know who she's looking for. 'I could tell from her voice on the phone,' she says. 'I can always tell if they're Vietnamese. Their English sounds Chinese, but Vietnamese people sound a little different and they have beautiful skin, really light.'

A woman in high-heeled sandals, tight trousers and a white top with sequins appears, holding her mobile phone. She seems to be looking for someone too. 'Are you Mona?' she asks Lom.

I wonder about the name, but don't say anything. Lom has used a lot of different names since we've known each other, always for a good reason. She knows when it's good to use a pseudonym. 'Hurry up and follow me,' says Vee. Then, nodding in my direction, she asks Lom, 'Who's that?'

'She's just my friend,' says Lom. 'She's OK.'

Vee has long, bleached hair, precisely drawn eyebrows and her nails are alternately yellow, red, blue, purple and green, with delicate artificial gems affixed. They glitter in the sunshine when she moves her fingers. Lom tells me, 'It's because it's a secret nail and eyelash salon, so she doesn't want anyone to see us. The salon is in her apartment and it's not registered, so she doesn't have to pay taxes.'

I'm wondering if my presence makes this more risky, but I can't just disappear. 'Is it better if I don't go with you?' I ask.

'No, no, it's all right,' says Lom. 'We just have to get into the building.' I have to trust that it's OK she brings me along. When there is an actual risk of being discovered, I am usually told that I should leave because I stick out.

Vee takes us up to the sixth floor and into her one-room apartment. Two old doors have been adjoined to form a wall separating Vee's double bed from the lash bed, on which Lom lies down. There is a small yellow suitcase on the dressing table. In all the little migrant rooms I have visited, there is always a suitcase. Next to the table is a microphone and recording equipment. It looks like a mini-studio.

'Do you use that?' I ask.

'Yes,' says Vee. 'I sing and I record it.'

Lom asks Vee how much she makes. Vee says, 'I have about six clients per day and I get 150 dirham[37] per client. There are lots of clients; so many girls here need eyelashes.'

Lom calculates Vee's daily income. About £170. 'That's a good income,' says Lom, nodding at me. 'I've thought about doing nails and eyelashes,' she says. 'There are always clients.' I sense that Lom is impressed by how Vee has arranged this; how she has her own place, and is pretty, and sings.

Vee turns on thumping pop music and starts working on Lom's eyelashes, while explaining to Lom what

[37] 31 GBP

she's doing. It is as if she is teaching her. First, a bit of glue on the tweezers and then you attach three hairs at a time. Vee is efficient and precise, but there are a lot of hairs to glue on. When Lom's eyelashes are done, she thanks Vee. 'I'll be back,' she says.

We walk to the Starbucks in Al Muraqqabat, which has become our usual meeting place. Lom orders a sweet green chai with whipped cream. 'What name should I put on the cup?' asks the server.

'Mona,' says Lom.

'Why Mona?' I ask.

All she says is, 'That's my work name. In Dubai, my name is Mona.'

We sit down. I drink my coffee and Lom eats her whipped cream with a spoon. 'My cat loves whipped cream,' she says. Lom has already told me a lot about her cat in the few days we have been together. It was given to her by her boyfriend, whom I haven't met. His father is from Saudi Arabia and his mother is Emirati. He is a black Muslim, twenty-five years old and he works as a security guard. He doesn't know what Lom does for work. Or she doesn't think he knows.

At first, Lom didn't like the cat. She lives in a small apartment with four women from Myanmar, who came to Dubai looking for work. She has a mini-room without a window, where there is only space for her bed, a TV and her suitcase. But now there is a litter box too. One day, she dropped her phone between the bed and the wall and she couldn't fit her hand down to get it. But the cat crept under the bed and meowed at the phone, so she knew where to reach in and get it. 'After that, I loved the cat,' she says. 'It was like she was trying to help me. It only wants to be with me and it meows when I leave.'

I go with Lom back to her place. 'I live on a pretty horrible street,' she says. 'Twice when I came home at night, around three, in the dark, alone, a man was standing here by this door' – she points as we walk past – 'jerking off. So horrible. I said to the guy, "I don't want to see that." He just seemed crazy, so I didn't really get scared.' She laughs. 'But then again, I see dicks all the time at work. So I don't want to see them when I'm off.'

Couples Massage

In Dubai, it is not always obvious where a person can buy sex. Lom's workplace is a hotel; inside the hotel is a spa, which is actually a brothel. I want to see where she works, but I can't just walk in and say that I'm an anthropologist and I'd like to see their brothel. And I can't just say that I'm 'Mona's friend. I have to pay for the time 'Mona' spends with me. That's how it works. Lom says the best way for me to see the place is to book a massage for me and Janus. Then Lom and her Thai friend will give us massages without 'extra service'.

Lom books two slots for us at eleven at night. Janus is instructed not to ask about Lom's friend's job – that she sells sex and offers extra service. Lom has only told her friend, who is a skilled massage therapist and sex worker, that Janus and I are friends she met a long time ago in Thailand. Janus is a bit uneasy about the situation: that he will be alone with a sex worker in a shady hotel so that I can talk with Lom in the next room. But he has come along with me numerous times on my fieldwork and he agrees. I withdraw 1,200 dirham[38] from a cash machine in the hotel. Two hundred dirham[39] goes to the owner of the brothel and Lom and her girlfriend split the rest.

Janus and I take the lift up and find 'the spa'. The

[38] 244 GBP
[39] 41 GBP

entrance is decorated with orange and yellow tropical flowers and the aroma of incense streams out into the otherwise seedy hall. We ask for Mona. Lom appears in a tight-fitting turquoise outfit with three gold stripes on the sleeves, like a stewardess impersonator. Lom's friend takes Janus to her space and I follow Lom.

Lom locks the door from inside and we sit on the bed. There is a bouquet of yellow plastic flowers lying on a white disposable sheet. Coloured lightbulbs give off red, pink and purple light. There are plastic bottles with oil, lotion and hand sanitiser. She tells me that the little bags with disposable shorts are for the clients, so they don't get oil on their underwear. The wallpaper is loose along the edge of the bed. The room looks worn.

In the next room, Janus is lying there getting a massage by an experienced sex worker. Lom says that she already gave her the 500, as we agreed. 'That way she won't be unsure about her pay and offer him extra service anyway,' she says, very businesslike. As if it goes without saying that Janus would not be able to say no if he were asked. I think that there are probably not many wives who have sent their husbands to get a massage from a sex worker so she can learn more about sex work.

I ask Lom, 'How was it to return to this work after being home with your kids and your sick mother in the village? You were wondering if you could do it again.'

'I get angry at the clients more easily now,' she says, 'if they take more than I want to give, more than they paid for. I am clearer about what I'm willing to do. I have to be a bitch once in a while. Maybe because

I'm taking hormones to control my period. If they try to touch my breasts, I get all . . .' Lom closes her eyes and puts her hands up in front of her breasts as if in disgust. 'There was an Indian man who wanted a massage and then he wanted extra service, but he would only pay 50 dirham[40] for the ending. That was what he said he had. But it costs twice as much as that. So I said, "If you don't have the money, you'll have to leave." He was also icky and he smelled, so I was happy to get rid of him. He told me, "That's too expensive for you. I thought you were cheap." So I threw him out.

'Sometimes, a Pakistani man comes by and brings me food. He drives all the way across town with Thai food. He doesn't want to have sex, he just brings me the food and we sit and talk. The receptionist lets him, because of the food.

'I am trying more often not to have real sex. Hand jobs are better at my age. I feel too old for all that other stuff. I give them a massage and a happy ending. I am tired of sex after all these years doing this work. I'm not interested in sex.' She adds, a bit apologetically, 'I mean, I do it with my boyfriend; you have to, so then I give it a bit of drama.'

I hear the door next to our room open and Janus' voice. They're done, so we go out too. Janus smells like massage oil. When we leave, I say, 'Thanks, Mona.'

We go to Bollywood Rocks, a bar in the cellar beneath Lom's hotel, where a group of women dance alluringly on a stage. Groups of Indian men watch and when a beautiful belly dancer in a red dress enters, the men applaud and shout excitedly. She dances seductively in front of them. We try to guess which countries the

[40] 10 GBP

women are from. We think they're from Iran, India and Pakistan.

We walk to a more expensive hotel. A Filipina trans woman is sitting on a barstool alone on the stage, singing Celine Dion's cover of 'All by Myself'. She does look lonesome in a flowery dress, exuding untold stories. Three women with long, black wavy hair are sitting alone at the bar in tight dresses and high heels. They are smoking cigarettes and looking at their phones. Otherwise, only Janus and I are in the bar. There are no clients for them. I remember Lom's description: 'We are extra room service.'

On the way back to our own hotel, there are six women on the street looking for clients. They look like Nigerians from Benin City: they have tattoos on their faces and I recognise their accents. The women in Nigeria have told me that they travel to Dubai for work now, because travelling to Europe is so difficult and so expensive.

My Father Loves Me Now

'Will you help me book a ticket to Thailand?' Lom asks me.

We are sitting in our usual corner of Starbucks and Lom has her green drink with extra whipped cream. I am leaving Dubai and there is a feeling of trying to accomplish all we can with the time we have left. Earlier, we spoke about her being away for three years during the pandemic and that now she would like to take a brief trip back home to see her children. She has also paid an expensive private doctor in Dubai to find out why she has pain and bleeding in her uterus. He scanned her and said there are some fibroids that he can remove, but she can't afford to be operated on in Dubai. So she has been taking hormone pills for several months to interrupt her menstruation; that way she can keep working. In Thailand, she can be seen for free at the local hospital and perhaps be operated on at the hospital at Khorat. If she is going to keep seeing clients, she will have to have her fibroids removed in Thailand.

'I'm nervous about writing my name wrong,' she says, 'and that I will run into so many problems when I want to travel back to Dubai. It has to be a direct flight – Dubai to Bangkok round trip. That way, I run into fewer police who can ask questions. And I found a cheaper flight earlier today, so maybe you could help me book it now?'

In a way, I am surprised that she's asking me. Of all

the women I have met, Lom is the one who has travelled the most to find work. She has been in England, Malaysia, South Korea and now Dubai. But when I think more about it, in almost every instance someone else has paid for her ticket. The decision to travel has always been her own, but other people have arranged it or paid for it.

'Do you have money for a return ticket?' I ask.

'Yes,' she says. 'I have some money now and I also borrowed some from "a lady".'

'OK,' I say, 'I can give you some of the money for the ticket too. It's better that you don't go too deep into debt.'

'Thanks. It's going to be expensive to go back to Thailand,' says Lom, 'because I have to buy school uniforms for my kids and a lot of people think I can help them with all kinds of things because I'm working in Dubai. And I want to take MJ and BM on a trip to Pattaya for a few days, to swim at the beach. My boyfriend says that he'll pay my rent here in Dubai and take care of my cat while I'm in Thailand.'

We walk over and sit on one of the benches that circle the central plaza in Al Muraqqabat. It is getting dark and the plaza is filling with people. There are migrants selling water, jewellery and lighters. A couple of boys are dribbling a ball. We buy takeaway food from one of the many Iranian restaurants.

'What do you think your plan will be after your trip to Thailand?' I ask.

'I'll have to come back to Dubai and work for two or three years, but I want to go back to my children. MJ is almost a teenager. She needs her mother and shouldn't be growing up with just her old grandfather. My father is doing what he can, but he is no mother. MJ is already acting like a teen, interested in how she looks and boys and all kinds of activities. She gives me a headache all the way over in Dubai. I haven't been working and been away from her for so many years so that she will end up in the same kind of work as me. I want to find another way to earn money back in my village, be with my kids and give them an education. Maybe I could learn to do manicures and eyelashes, just like Vee.'

Lom looks straight ahead, as if she is trying to see into the future. 'I've also talked with someone I know in Denmark at a parlour,' she says. 'But it costs 60,000 euros[41] to go to Denmark and I would have to perform all kinds of sex, and I don't want to do that any more.'

Lom has sold sex since she was sixteen, only interrupted by the periods when she was home in her village, when she had MJ and BM and the time when she cared for her sick mother. Now she's thirty-seven. She has sold sex for fourteen years. This is the first time I have heard her talk seriously about giving it up.

'My father and I are doing better,' she says. 'It changed when I got divorced, my mother died and I came to Dubai and was able to send a lot of money home. My father has respect for me and he has started asking if I am OK. Sometimes he even calls me and says he gets worried if I don't pick up the phone. When I got Covid, he was nervous and called me all the time. He sees me as a grown woman now.

'I just want to stay here long enough to renovate my father's house and hold a one-hundred-days-after-party in my mother's memory. My relationship to her was complicated, you know, but I miss her. It is over

[41] 52,631 GBP

a hundred days since she died, but we never had the party that you're supposed to and I want to give that to her.'

'I know,' I say, 'she meant a lot to you. We actually haven't talked about your mother since the funeral. Do you remember crying out for your mother's hand?'

'I do,' says Lom. 'I thought she looked angry, so unhappy there in the coffin. Everything was so sad. She wouldn't let go. She didn't want to die. She was still young.'

'My mother didn't want to die either,' I say. 'She was too young too.' I tell Lom about the dream I had about my mother, who was no longer able to get the wasps out of my hair.

'I see my mother too. I see her in the house in the village back home and here in my room in Dubai. But she always looks angry. She didn't let go before she died. She carries a grudge; she's bitter. She's filled with the bad things that happened in her life.

'Do you remember when she travelled to Pattaya with Sommai? But my mother couldn't deal with the work and she returned home with my father. Then Sommai met Niels in Pattaya and had a good life in Denmark. But my father was not good to my mother in the years that followed. He was unfaithful and he wasted money gambling. I think she felt that she wasted her life on him. And she never forgave him.

'With all that anger, my mother became very agitated before she died. She lay in the hospital yelling out her anger. She wrapped her oxygen hose around her neck and tried to strangle herself. She was completely filled up with anger, jealousy and bitterness.

But you have to be cleansed within in order to move on after death. I feel so sad when I see my mother here in Dubai at night with her angry face.'

I realise that both of our mothers yelled out on their deathbeds. For different reasons. But they yelled out.

Everything is Just an Illusion

A couple of months later, Lom calls me from Thailand. 'I'm glad to be back together with my kids,' she says, 'but it's more complicated to be home than I thought.' We have our cameras on and I can see that she is sitting in the yard in front of her father's house. 'My kids have grown up since I was away. I don't want to leave them again. I usually get bored after visiting my village, and I want to get away, but not this time. Now I just want to stay here with them or find someplace closer where I can work. Dubai is too far away and the travelling back and forth is too expensive.

'My kids need me now. MJ is mad at me because her father told her that I am the kind of mother who just leaves. That she can't count on me. I have tried to explain that I've been travelling to earn money for her life here.

'The woman living next door, who has been a sex worker in Germany, teased BM and told him that I was a hooker in Dubai. I had to talk with both MJ and BM. I told them I love them and that they shouldn't listen to what other people say about me. I explained how I support them and that I am taking care of them as well as I can. But MJ won't hug me any more. BM will, but he is very quiet. I can't figure out how he is.

'It has been expensive to come back home. The kids needed school uniforms, new bags and books. MJ is preoccupied with how she looks. She uses my make-up and my clothes. She wants to go to the city and buy things. She says we need to buy cream so we can scrub her skin and lighten it.'

Three months later, Lom is back in Dubai. She posts a mirror selfie in a lift with a glitter filter on Facebook, wearing a short top and tight trousers in a lift on the way to work. Underneath, she writes, 'Love is not real. Everything is just an illusion. No one belongs to anyone. When the time is up, we all have to leave. In the end, we have to be with ourselves.'

Aperol Spritz

Sicily, 2023

Towards the end of April 2023, I travel back to Sicily to visit Vivian. I want to read the chapters in this book aloud to her, so I can be sure to have captured her story correctly and to make sure that she wants me to use it. Because of Covid and Wilder's birth, we have not seen each other in three years.

She asks when I'm landing. I tell her 2.15 p.m. When I turn on my phone after landing in Catania, there is a text from her: 'I took the bus to pick you up, but your plane was late so I had to go back home.' The thought that she used her only day off to come to the airport to get me is a surprise that warms my heart and makes me feel happy. She didn't have to do that.

But she wasn't able to wait for my plane, which was an hour late, because she didn't want to get back too late to pick up Kindys and then be at her new job, where she is caring for an old woman. Everything in her life is precarious. She is always on the brink of being unemployed, afraid of Kindys being taken from her, having her visa recalled and being deported. Just because she wants to pick me up from the airport.

I text back that everything is fine and that I'm sorry she came out for nothing. When I arrive by taxi at the hotel, she is standing there at the entrance. She had just enough time to pick up Kindys and take him to football and now there she is waiting for me.

'Where's the baby?' she asks. 'Why didn't you bring

your baby for me? Is it only you?' She looks a bit disappointed. She takes my bag and carries it into the hotel. I follow her. I would actually rather carry my luggage myself, but she receives me like a helpful friend. One man is watering the dry lawn out front; another is cleaning the swimming pool.

The receptionist looks at Vivian and appears to wonder about our relationship to one another. Vivian is proud and undismayed. She is the one who can speak Italian to the receptionist, not me.

'I'm going up to put my things in my room,' I say.

'Go ahead,' says Vivian. 'Get freshened up and then we'll go out.' She sits in the reception area and waits for me. I enter the lift and hope she doesn't attract too many stares.

We go into town with Kindys to have pizza and gelato. We order an Aperol spritz to celebrate that Vivian just received a two-year visa to remain in Italy, the longest period she has ever been granted. This is so that Kindys can keep going to his Italian school and so that she can stay here and take care of him. Without Kindys, she would have been sent back to Nigeria.

Money Puts a Stop to All the Nonsense

A young woman comes over to us in the restaurant and places a yellow parakeet on Vivian's head and a green parakeet on her hand. We laugh and take photos.

The young woman says, 'Fifteen euros.'[42] We were naive not to understand that we had to pay to take photos of her birds. Vivian stares at her in disbelief. 'That's fraud,' she says, indignantly. 'You have to tell us beforehand. And fifteen euros is ludicrous. That's way too much.' She looks at me, as if she's nervous that I think it was her responsibility to check, since she's the Italian speaker. I take out fifteen euros and say that it's all right. We can't do anything about it now. 'But Sine,' says Vivian, 'fifteen euros for two birds in my hair. That's almost what I make in a full day.'

The young woman leaves with her birds. 'How much do you earn in a day?' I ask her.

'Twenty-two euros,'[43] she says, 'to be on call twenty-four hours. That's how I got my visa. I had to be with Kindys and I had to have a job. So I had to accept what they offered. I was living in that private camp, you know.'

I nod. This is a situation where a family receives money from the government for having refugees living with them. 'A woman offered to take me from the camp if I would care for her eighty-four-year-old mother, and cook, clean and do laundry.

[42] 13 GBP
[43] 19 GBP

'So that's where Kindys and I are living now. We share a room in the old lady's apartment. We wrote in the contract that I would work twenty-five hours a week for 700 euros.[44] Twenty-five hours was enough to get a residency visa. I work every day of the week, except Thursday, when I am off between 8 a.m. and 8 p.m. The lady is very old. She can't go to the toilet by herself and she calls on me several times every night. Then she wakes Kindys and there I am with two children. I always take care of Kindys first; he's my child after all. I can't leave during the day and I have to be home every night. I get no vacation. The old lady eats my Nigerian food, even though she's supposed to eat her Italian food. I have my own food that I paid for myself. But she eats it and then I'm hungry. But I can't do anything about it. The daughter, whose mother I am taking care of, thinks I should be grateful that she took me out of the camp. But they treat me like their slave.' Vivian sighs. 'They always find a way to exploit us.'

'So you're saying,' I say, 'that you get twenty-two euros per day to be constantly available? Seven euros more than having two birds in your hair.'

Vivian laughs and says, 'That's right. Maybe I should buy two parakeets.' She goes on, 'But I send 500 euros[45] to my family in Nigeria each month. I have to take care of my mother – even though I haven't spoken with her in five years. I have to, because I am the second daughter. My big sister is taking care of my parents back home and also my sons. So I have to earn money.'

'So, how many people are you supporting?' I ask.

[44] 607 GBP
[45] 433 GBP

She counts on her fingers. 'My mother, my father, my kids, my sister, their children ... eleven people,' she says, resigned. 'And we are building a house. Have you seen it?'

I haven't. She pulls out her phone and shows me a photo of a tan house that looks nearly finished, but also seems old and dingy already. It has iron bars in the windows and a muddy yard. 'This is how far we have gotten with my money. We can only have work done on it when I have sent money for the next phase. It's expensive to build – it uses up all my money.

'Sometimes I turn off my phone so all of them in Nigeria can't ask me for more money. Just to have a minute of peace. But my family back home looks up to me. They love me more, now that I'm helping them. They respect me. The money brings respect. Money puts a stop to all the nonsense.'

A Spot on Her Forehead

On my last day in Sicily, it's grey and windy. Vivian is going to shop in Lidl for the old lady after taking Kindys to school at 8 a.m. She has forty-five minutes free before the lady starts calling and asking where she is. I meet her at her front door, so we can walk together with Kindys to his school and then to Lidl, and squeeze every second out of the time we have to say goodbye. Vivian is not allowed to have guests at the apartment, so we have to meet outside.

We drop off Kindys with hugs goodbye. He is the only black boy in a school of white Italians. 'Look at him,' says Vivian. 'He's all alone here. I'd like to find other African children he can play with, but it's not easy when we have to be at home with the lady all the time. During summer vacation, he has two months off, but he ends up sitting in a dark room with his iPad. I don't get vacation and I'll get fired if I ask for time off. I can't give him what he needs . . .

'Come on,' she says, 'let's hurry. I only need a few things, but I will tell the old lady there was a long line. Then we might have time for a coffee and saying goodbye.'

We hurry off to Lidl and she buys tomatoes and pasta and I buy a jar of Nutella for Kindys. 'He'll need some bread with that,' says Vivian, and we hurry to find it. 'The lady is going to think it strange that I can afford Nutella,' she says. 'She looks in my bags when I come home.'

'Is it better if I don't buy it?' I ask.

'No,' says Vivian, 'Kindys will be so happy. I'll say I got it from my girlfriend.'

We have twenty-five minutes left and we sit down at a little coffee shop next to Lidl's car park. 'Thank you for telling me about your life and for going over all my notes with me,' I say. 'When the book comes out, I hope you will come to Denmark.'

'I will come,' says Vivian, 'and maybe stay there.' She laughs. 'As you see, I have my own life here in Italy, but I want to live more independently and make my own decisions, and bring my two boys over from Nigeria.'

'Are you dating anyone?' I ask. I know she has been talking with a man from Catania. 'No,' says Vivian. 'I love my children and no one else.'

Then I ask her, 'How long since you've seen them?'

She thinks for a moment. 'I left them in 2013 – so, I haven't seen my children in ten years.' The air seems to condense and she goes quiet, fidgeting with her glass. She gets tears in her eyes. I've never seen that happen before.

'Ten years!' I say. 'Those boys have gotten big since you left.'

'I know,' she says. 'I asked them how they would be able to recognise me when I eventually make it back to Nigeria. They said, "We will look for the spot you have on your forehead." She points to a small beauty mark in the middle of her forehead. I never noticed it before. But now I know that is how her children will know who she is.

I have to leave to make my flight. 'Sine,' says Vivian, 'I have to ask you about something.' She looks right at me. 'You know I don't like asking you for anything.

But I am wondering if you would take care of Kindys this summer, take him with you on vacation, so I can work and he won't have to sit inside all summer with the old lady.'

'Yes,' I say.

Orange Life Vests

Italy, 2023

While I'm writing, Kindys is running around outside the holiday house with Ella and Wilder. They are blowing bubbles, playing football and eating Nutella sandwiches during breaks. At night, Kindys and Ella sleep in twin beds in the kids' room like siblings. Wilder walks in and gives them hugs in the morning. One of the first words he learned was 'Kindys'.

I FaceTime with Vivian every day and tell her how it's going. 'Can you teach him some more English?' she asks. 'He only speaks Italian. Pretty soon he won't be able to talk with his brothers in Nigeria. I speak English to him, but he only answers in Italian.'

'Sure,' I say. 'We speak English with him and he is starting to answer in English too.'

Another day, Vivian asks, 'Can you teach him to swim? I can't teach him. I'm afraid of the water, you know, so we don't go to the beach and we are always at home with the old lady.' In a worried mother's voice, she adds, 'But remember to give him arm floats so he doesn't drown.'

'Yes, I'll remember,' I say. 'We just bought arm floats for him.'

A few days later, we're at the beach. From the water's edge, Kindys runs over to me excitedly, water dripping off his body. He puts out his arms so I can take off his orange floats. His skin is cold, his lips bluish-white from playing in the water too long. I put my hands

The Summer of 2023 when Kindys, who crossed the Mediterranean in his mother's belly in 2014, joined the author and her family in Italy

around one float to slip it off. In a flash, I see an image of Kindys' face among thousands of orange life vests against dark skin. The wet bodies and bluish-white lips. I have seen these pictures all too often in my work.

I shake my head, try to get the image to vanish. I can't stand it, that my brain did that. I know he was out there on the sea inside Vivian's big belly. And that she wore an orange life vest, which she was unable to tie. And now he is here on the beach with the Mediterranean behind him. A child who just wants to play, swim and kick a football, with no thought of the drowning that he and his mother so narrowly escaped.

I remove the other float and wrap a towel around him. He lies down on the sun lounger and eats his sour cream and onion crisps. He is in the sunshine, eight years old, and so alive. I love this boy. He is so gentle, loving, fun and smart. He could have died. But he didn't. Someone rescued him from the sea. He is here and his skin is warming in the sun.

The Rescue Zone

A few days later, while I am still at the house in Italy with my family and Kindys, Doctors Without Borders calls me. They read something I wrote in the newspaper about the current situation in the Mediterranean, where thousands of migrants and refugees continue trying to cross into Europe every month. They would like to see if we could collaborate on what my research is finding out about the situation at sea.

Around that time, Doctors Without Borders is out in their rescue ship *Geo Barents* nearly every night, pulling people both with but most often without orange life vests out of the water. They often embark from Augusta in eastern Sicily, near Syracuse where Vivian lives, and near the Fascist monument, where Italy has honoured the Italian soldiers who died fighting over Africa.

Because they are rescuing migrants, Doctors Without Borders is being blamed for encouraging even more people to cross the sea and for assisting the traffickers. This is what they would like to talk with me about. I say that there is nothing in my research that indicates rescues cause more people to cross.

They are obviously frustrated over the situation. 'We have been ordered by the authorities,' they say, 'to only rescue one sinking boat at a time, even though there are sometimes several that have capsized in the course of a single stormy night. So we can only perform one rescue and then we have to sail far away from the rescue zone in the central Mediterranean. We are rarely permitted to let them off in Port Augusta or anywhere in Sicily; we have to sail far away to the north Italian ports. This means that people are drowning while we are sailing away from them.'

We talk more about the Doctors Without Borders mobile clinic, which operates in the mountains on the border between Italy and France, not far from where we are with Kindys. They meet a lot of women who have crossed the sea, but then end up in makeshift tents on the border. Some sell sex to survive. Some are pregnant.

After our conversation, I write in my notebook: 'People are being criminalised for selling sex or for crossing the border without documents. And the organisations that help them are too. Doctors are being accused of human trafficking.'

Doctors Without Borders invites me out on *Geo Barents* to see their work in the Mediterranean. Out on the sea where Vivian and Kindys were rescued. The sea Becky wanted to cross so badly, but which also terrified her. I want to go.

Proud

I have been through all of my notebooks. Vivian is in Sicily where, after nearly ten years, she has received a two-year residency visa. She is hoping that, eventually, the work she is doing for the old Italian woman will allow her to bring her two other children from Nigeria to Italy.

Lom is in Dubai, hoping that she will earn enough in the years ahead to retire from being a sex worker, learn to apply eyelashes and stay home with her children.

Becky is dead.

I call up Sommai in Thy. 'What do you think the end of your story should be in the book?' I ask her.

'I don't know. What do you think?'

'What is the most important thing that is happening in your life right now?'

She thinks about it. 'I don't know, Sine. There's not much happening. I'm just here in Thy.'

'I saw on Facebook,' I say, 'that you had a visit from Pen.'

'Yes, she was just here, living with me for three weeks with food and everything. Her first time in Denmark.'

'I saw when Pen posted a photo and wrote, "Thanks to Sommai for my good visit to Denmark," and I could not help but think that she was the rich one who wouldn't lend you five kilos of rice, back when you were poor. And that was the final humiliating thing that made you leave for Pattaya. That's what I remember you saying. And now you were able to host her in Denmark in your and Niels' house.

'Maybe that is a kind of ending. That you have arrived at a place in your life where you are someone who can invite others to your home, even the richest woman from your village.'

'Yes, that was really nice to be able to do that. But it wasn't because I wanted to puff myself up or say "Look at me now, I'm such an important lady." I don't feel that I am above her.'

'No, I know that,' I say.

It's quiet on the phone for a little while, then Sommai continues, 'But I did talk about this with some of my Thai friends, because they could remember when she wouldn't lend me rice back then. She often said no. Not just that one time. But she was a wonderful guest, very gracious. And we said that it might inspire her, that I invited her to Denmark as my guest. That a person can give something back – even to those who once snubbed you.'

'So maybe that could be your ending?' I say.

'It could, but I don't think my ending should be about Pen.'

'OK, then let me ask in another way. When you look back on your life, back when you went to Pattaya, meeting Niels and your life here in Denmark, how do you feel?'

'Proud,' says Sommai immediately. 'I feel proud.'

I know how she will answer, because she has told me many times before, but I ask anyway: 'Proud in what way?'

'I am proud of myself and of what I've done. Because it changed my life. And it changed the lives of my children. They are doing well in Denmark now. We are doing well.'

'Would you say you are at peace with your life?'

'Yes. I don't want to move back to Thailand anymore. After being there for a while, I miss Denmark and I want to come back. I don't mind if I die in Denmark. I am in both places, in Thailand and in Denmark.'

I imagine that she is sitting where she has sat so many times when we have talked – in her kitchen, with the view of the fields and the Thy windmills, with a cup of coffee in front of her. Suddenly I miss her.

'That's the way it is, Sine.'

Sommai at a bar in Pattaya

Notes

i Names of people and places have been removed or changed where this has been deemed necessary. Sommai, Lom, Becky and Vivian and the names of their families have not been altered, with their permission. Becky appeared before her death in the documentary *Becky's Journey* (2014), directed by Sine Plambech. (Available on Vimeo.) Information about Becky's life which appears in this book also appeared in this film, as well as in *Points of Departure* (2014), Sine Plambech's PhD thesis, which Becky approved before her death. The family members of Sine Plambech who appear in this book approved their depictions.

ii Plambech, Sine. 2010. '"My body is my piece of land": Indebted deportation among undocumented migrant sex workers from Thailand and Nigeria in Europe.' *Security Dialogue*. Also see: *Center mod Menneskehandels Årsrapport*. 2022. [*Danish Centre Against Human Trafficking Annual Report*. 2022]. (Available from Center mod Menneskehandel.) This report does not contain a summary of the number of sex workers in Denmark, but of migrants questioned for trafficking, of which Thai nationals were the largest group in 2022, and Nigerians the next largest. This was the reverse of previous results, and keeps changing due to various dynamics, laws and travel routes.

iii Piot, Charles. 2010. *Nostalgia for the Future: West Africa after the Cold War.* Chicago University Press.

iv Mintz, Sidney W. 1985. *Sweetness and Power: The Place of Sugar in Modern History*. Penguin Books.

v Klein, Naomi. 1999. *No Logo: Taking Aim at the Brand Bullies*. Knopf Canada.

vi Saviano, Roberto. 2015. *Zero Zero Zero*. Translated by Virginia Jewiss. Allen Lane.

vii LOKK (Landsorganisation af kvindekrisecentre). 2003. *Når drømme og håb forvandles til mareridt: En rapport om danske mænds vold mod udenlandske kvinder og børn.* Finansieret af Ministeriet for flygtninge, indvandrere og integration & OAK Foundation. (2003). [LOKK (Danish National Crisis Center for Women). 2003. 'When dreams and hope turn into a nightmare: A report on Danish men's violence against foreign-born women and children.' Financed by the Ministry of Refugees, Immigration and Integration & the OAK Foundation.]

viii Boontawee, Kampoon. 1987. *A Child of the Northeast.* Kled Thai Co.

ix Parts of this chapter and the next appeared in the documentary film *Trafficking* (2010), directed by Sine Plambech and Judith Lansade. (Available on Filmstriben.)

x '12 ludere fængslet efter razzia.' *Ekstra Bladet.* Copenhagen, Denmark. 2 April 2009. ['Twelve Prostitutes Jailed After Raid.']

xi Aligwo, Leo. 'The Lure of the International Sex Trade.' *The Post Express.* Lagos, Nigeria. 8 August 1999.

xii International Organization for Migration (IOM). 2017. *UN Migration Agency Issues Report on Arrivals of Sexually Exploited Migrants, Chiefly from Nigeria. IOM Report.* (Available at: iom.int/news/un-migration-agency-issues-report-arrivals-sexually-exploited-migrants-chiefly-nigeria)

xiii Akhigbe, Allwell Oseahume and Efetobor, Stephanie Effevottu. 2023. *For the Greater Good: The Economic and Social Impacts of Irregular Migration on Families in Benin City, Nigeria.* In: *Forced Migration and Separated Families (IMISCOE Research Series).* Edited by Marja Tiilikainen, Johanna Hiitola, Abdirashid A. Ismail and Jaana Palander. Springer.

Plambech, Sine. 2017. 'Sex, Deportation and Rescue: Economics of Migration among Nigerian Sex Workers.' *Feminist Economics* 23:3. 134–159.

xiv Plambech, Sine & Cold-Ravnkilde, Signe Marie. 2015. 'Boko Haram: From Local Grievances to Violent Insurgency.' Danish Institute for International Studies. DIS Report 21. (Available at: https://pure.diis.dk/ws/portalfiles/portal/461691/DIIS_Report_21_Boko_Haram_WEB.pdf)

xv Dabiri, Emma. 2021. *What White People Can Do Next: From Allyship to Coalition.* Penguin Books.

xvi *19 Love Theatre* was produced by the theatre company Fix+Foxy and played from 2–23 May 2015.

xvii Raufu, Abiodun. 2002. 'Unsafe Abortions Cause 20,000 Deaths a Year in Nigeria.' *BMJ* 325:7371. 988. (Available at: https://pmc.ncbi.nlm.nih.gov/articles/PMC1169586/)

xviii Global Media Insight. 2023. 'UAE Population Statistics 2023.' (Available at: https://www.globalmediainsight.com/blog/uae-population-statistics/)

Some of the photographs featured in this book, as well as Sommai's and Lom's stories, were used in the film documentaries *Fra Thailand til Thy 1-4* (2008) [*Love on Delivery* (2008)], directed by Janus Metz and based on Sine Plambech's research, and *Hjertelandet* (2018) [*Heartbound* (2018)], directed by Janus Metz and Sine Plambech. (Accessible on Filmstriben.)

Acknowledgements

Thanks to:

Sommai, Lom, Vivian and Becky
Julius, Carl, Ella and Wilder
Janus Metz
My parents and siblings
Morten Alsinger
Sara Cirkeline Dornonville de la Cour Nygaard
Lucia Odoom
Aphinya Jatuparisakul
Lilie Chouliaraki
Ninna Nyberg Sørensen
Marie Bruvik Heinskou
Janne Breinholt Bak
Peter Øvig Knudsen
Daniel Robert Andersen
Marlene Diemar
Steven Sampson
Stenbroens Jurister – Maja Løvbjerg Hansen and Nadir Kadhim Hamza Sawitree Puangkrathok
Busayo Iruemiobe
Chinedum Maxzy Iregbu
Funlola
Ying
Yale University, The Ethnicity, Race and Migration Program

London School of Economics and Political Science, Department of Media and Communications
Dansk Institut for Internationale Studier

And to all the sex workers, migrants, street people, and many others, who have shared their stories with me.

Also translated by Michael Favala Goldman

Dependency, Tove Ditlevsen, Penguin Classics

The Trouble with Happiness, Tove Ditlevsen, Penguin Classics

The Starveling, Cecil Bødker, Spuyten Duyvil Press

Something To Live Up To: Selected Poems of Benny Andersen, Benny Anderson, Spuyten Duyvil Press

Out of the Blue, Rebecca Back-Lauritsen and Anna Margrethe Kjærgaard, Enchanted Lion Books

Akoya Publishing
222 Kensal Road, London, W10 5BN

First published in Danish as *Global Sex:
Hvad sexarbejdere ved om kærlighed og kapitalisme*
by Hans Reitzels Forlag.

First published in the English language
by Akoya Publishing Ltd in 2026.
Published by agreement with Gyldendal Group Agency.

Paperback ISBN 978-1-83675-006-2
Ebook ISBN 978-1-83675-032-1

Design by Holly Titchener
Text design by Phil Cleaver
Typeset in 10/13pt Egizio URW by Six Red Marbles
UK, Thetford, Norfolk
Printed and bound in Lithuania by BALTO print

MIX
Paper | Supporting
responsible forestry
FSC
www.fsc.org
FSC® C013604

1 3 5 7 9 10 8 6 4 2

The authorised representative in the EEA is eucomply
OÜ Pärnu mnt 139b-14 11317 Tallinn, Estonia.
hello@eucompliancepartner.com
+337 576 90241

A CIP record for this book is available
from the British Library.

akoyapublishing.com